God's
Sovereignty
Starring
YOU

Kimberly Ann Jones

IN PRINT™

Published by:
Grace in Print Publications
Shreveport, Louisiana

To contact the author, visit:
EzekielsChristianMinistries.com

To my Father, my Lord Jesus, and the Holy Spirit:

Out of cheerful obedience, I dedicate this book to you.

"For in him we live, and move, and have our being..." Acts 17:28

Advancing his kingdom,

Kimberly Ann Jones

Contents

Acknowledgments

There are so many people that God, my Father, has surrounded me with all of my growing up years and into and through my adult life. I wasn't going to write an "Acknowledgments" page because I could fill an entire book on all the family and friends that have been an intricate part of who I am today. However, I feel the unction to share my gratitude in the writing of this book to acknowledge those directly involved in this process.

To my Father, Jesus Christ, and the Holy Spirit: I humbly thank you for giving me the assignment to write this book. Thank you for prompting me to share our relationship with others.

To my husband, Harold, my "Boaz": You rescued me and gave me all that you are and all that you have. You taught me how to pursue the Lord through his word. You have allowed me to grow into the woman of God that I am today. Your love, strength, and courage is my anchor in this life that we share together.

To my son, TC: Your life initiated my hunger to know more about our Father based on his word. You taught me what it means to have childlike faith, and how to see and experience Jesus in the eyes of my heart.

To my friend and editor, Genevieve Schmitt: God brought us together on this journey. Your friendship, gifts, time, and encouragement have been invaluable. You prophesied over me at a Christian women's conference in New Albany, Ohio, and you were with me at another women's conference in Tomball, Texas, when I knew I was to engage the process of writing this book. The journey has begun!

To my friend, illustrator, photographer, and publisher, Dave Chesak: To watch your gifts in action has been a privilege. Unspeakable fascination emerges when I watch you create a masterpiece. Whether it is painting, making greeting cards, designing a logo, or creating this book cover, you are a joy to know and work with.

To my Tuesday and Wednesday Kingdom Sweetness Bible study groups: Thank you for being disciples, friends, and encouragers as I teach what Jesus has taught me.

To all my family and friends: thank you for your love and support.

Foreword

Most of us have heard the saying that, "It's the journey, not the destination." Well, no more is that statement true than when riding a motorcycle—yes, a motorcycle, where one's journey is not hampered by the walls of a car, but rather is heightened by having all five senses in touch with the surrounding environment. The seat of a motorcycle is where I've spent most of my adult years. The Lord blessed me with a career where I could combine my passions for motorcycle riding and exploration, with my professional skills of writing, storytelling, and copy editing. Most of the motorcycle-related articles I've penned focused on the journey, because that is where the wonder and the magic happens. For me, the getting from point A to point B has been what's provided the most magnificent memories in my life thus far.

Recently though, I shifted gears in my career where I've been able to spend more time with the Lord in prayer, more time meditating on his word, and more time humbly at his feet in his presence. And let me tell you, this journey, the one where I've allowed God to direct my steps, putting him in the center of every area of my life tops any motorcycle trip or adventure I've had to date. I've seen God do healing miracles in my life, financial miracles in my life, and I've had amazing breakthroughs in my marriage and other personal relationships.

When I invited God to get involved in the details the miracles began to happen. When I opened the door to allow God to step through that's when things really got exciting, and I've had a pretty exciting life up to this point already. Nothing—no amount of money, no amount of notoriety, no amount of worldly influence—tops a life with God directing one's steps. This book, *God's Sovereignty Starring YOU*, is your roadmap and your manuscript for navigating in a fresh new way the incredible journey that God has planned for you. The guidelines set forth in this book on how to hear from God directly and know that it is him has been a game changer for me in my spiritual journey!

Up until two years ago, the compass navigating my Christian walk included reading Christian books on spiritual growth, digesting a morning devotional or two, attending Christian conferences, surfing through teachings on YouTube, and church-hopping until I found the right combination of music and message that resonated for that season in my life. Oh, and I'd pick up the Bible occasionally hoping that the verse the book would fall open to would speak to me in that moment. I putt-putted along in my spiritual life gleaning bits and pieces and seeing some fruit in the process.

While I was making gains in certain areas, i.e. loving others better, and being more kind, compassionate, and forgiving, I was still going around some of the same mountains and not seeing fruit in those areas. So back to the books and conferences and begging-God-for-answers prayers I'd go. My spiritual walk was akin to two steps forward, one step back.

Thank goodness I've had the sense to lean into gut feelings most of my life (which I now know was the Holy Spirit's promptings), and made the time to get in my car to drive the twenty minutes to town to meet Kimberly Ann Jones and her husband, Harold, at the encouragement of some mutual friends when the couple was visiting my hometown two years ago. I became fast friends with the Jones', and have since been participating in Kimberly Ann's weekly Bible studies by Skype—me in Montana, she in Louisiana.

I was drawn to Kimberly Ann's fresh way of approaching the Bible and applying God's word to everyday life. I'd never heard anyone teach this way before! When Kimberly Ann talks, she literally speaks God's word to you, stringing applicable Bible verse to applicable Bible verse to address whatever topic is being discussed without you even knowing it (unless you know God's word for yourself). And she does it in such a way that enlightens you, encourages you, and edifies you as a son or daughter of God. Then she backs up what she just shared with a testimony of how God's word, his promise, has played out in her own life. Kimberly Ann's journey is a testament to years of sowing God's word into her heart and then listening to the Holy Spirit so she knows the right thing to say or do that ministers grace to the hearer.

The Lord directed Kimberly Ann to write *God's Sovereignty Starring YOU*. She's been obedient to the assignment and I can tell you that it is literally a download from the Holy Spirit from her heart to yours, the reader. She includes the foundational parable, the Sower and the Seed from Mark 4. Never, ever in my entire Christian life has anyone told me to start here in my understanding of how to participate in God's sovereign plan. Understanding this parable is the key to your Bible reading time and everything falling into place.

Jesus told us in Mark 4:13, *"Know ye not this parable, and how then will ye know all parables?"* Parables are what Jesus used to teach us how his kingdom operates on the earth, and the part we have to play in it. For me, understanding this parable was the "aha" moment I needed that unlocked my understanding to how God's kingdom, his sovereignty, is supposed to play out while we are here on the earth, including my starring role in it. I remember praying some years ago, "Lord, I want to get to a point where I think of you every moment of every day, and that my life is a prayer where I pray without ceasing" (1 Thessalonians 5:17). I'm nearly there with the guidance of my friend Kimberly Ann Jones who's just a little further along on this journey.

I thank Kimberly Ann for letting me edit this incredible book that was given to her from the Holy Spirit. During my time reading each word and cross referencing each Bible verse, I literally felt God's anointing on my life with the presence of the Holy Spirit guiding my edit decisions as I worked through each chapter. I was in a bubble of grace, love, and joy as I moved from page to page. It's been a huge blessing for me to go through this experience, one that has left an indelible mark on my soul.

My prayer is that you carve out the time needed to read this book and do the application assignments at the end of each chapter. These assignments came from the Holy Spirit, and you will harvest from the Lord to the extent that you sow in the time with Him. The Bible says, *"...He is a rewarder of them that diligently seek him"* (Hebrews 11:6). God promises that he rewards us when we diligently seek him. And the neat thing about God is that he doesn't give to us just twofold, but he supplies us with his fruit in multiples when we sow his word into our hearts. Here are just a few verses that speak to that principle of God's kingdom: *"Grace and peace be **multiplied** to you through the knowledge of God and of Jesus our Lord..."* (2 Peter 1:2 emphasis added); *"Now unto him that is able to do **exceeding abundantly** all that we ask or think..."* (Ephesians 3:20 emphasis added); *"Whereby are given unto us **exceeding** *great and precious promises...*" (2 Peter 1:4 emphasis added); *"...I am come that they might have life, and that they might have it **more abundantly**"* (John 10:10 emphasis added).

May you be rewarded by having an increase in the knowledge of God and of Jesus our Lord, and that you become a partaker of his divine nature such that you crave more and more and more of him in your life. And then when your cup runs over and you dwell in the house of the Lord, you can't help but freely give to others what you have freely received. In Jesus' precious name, I pray, amen.

Taking territory for Christ,
Genevieve Schmitt
An ambassador of God's kingdom here on the earth
August 27, 2018

Preface

You have picked up my book, *God's Sovereignty Starring YOU,* and probably wonder who I am. By the world's system I am a wife, a mother, a business owner, co-founder of a ministry, and I have previously climbed a few rungs of the corporate ladder.

However, in God's "system" I am a born-again believer of Jesus Christ, sealed with the Holy Spirit of promise, a good soldier of Jesus Christ, a king, a priest, an ambassador, and many other things according to the word of God. The most endearing reality for me at this time in my journey is that I am a child of God Almighty through Jesus Christ.

I've known Jesus since I was a little girl, but I did not know him through his word in the Bible. The journey to know him based on his word began about thirteen years ago when my son was healed of a congenital heart defect, a condition that was going to require surgery. When he was miraculously healed without surgical intervention, I needed to know more about the One whom I professed as Savior, but had not made Lord of my life.

Along this journey, I'd often hear quotes like, "God is sovereign," or "God is in control," or "God allows things to happen." We've probably all said them in moments of tragedy, or lack of understanding of the God who sent his only begotten Son because he loved us. During these years of pursuing to know Him better, I concur that based on the definition of "sovereign," God is indeed:

1. Supreme in power; possessing supreme dominion; as a sovereign prince
2. Supreme; superior to all others; chief
3. Supremely efficacious; superior to all others; predominant; effectual

(*Webster's Dictionary 1828 - Online Edition,* s.v. "sovereign," accessed August 20, 2018, http://webstersdictionary1828.com/ Dictionary/sovereign)

In God's sovereignty though, he has given us a part to play in life. With humility and respect for this sovereignty, it's my heart's desire to fulfill the part he wants me to play in this "production" called life by being obedient to what he wants to accomplish through me, because of the high price that was paid for my salvation.

This book is only a glimpse into what little I know about him at this point in my journey and the finished work of the cross. Is it just for me to read my Bible and go to church, knowing that one day I get to go be with Jesus? Nope, not based on what I've read in his word, and learned from many who are revealing Jesus all over the world. In God's sovereignty, we all have a part to play in his will being done on the earth as it is in heaven. So, let's find out some of what God has told us regarding his part, our part, and the enemy's part in the big picture of life.

Several years back, a friend asked if I would put some scriptures together regarding a conversation that we had about our roles in God's plan. I told her that I would, but when the conversation was over, my first thought was, "Where do I begin?" I started to pray and ask the Holy Spirit for help. It was during this time searching for his wisdom and the applicable scriptures that I wrote a booklet. I sent my friend a handful of copies and then, prompted by the Holy Spirit, I began giving them out to individuals I was ministering to in stores, gas stations, and restaurants.

Last year, another friend told me that it was time for me to publish the booklet. This was the second confirmation that I was given that God wanted me to write this book. So, out of obedience to my Father, I am writing this book. Before you continue on, please stop and ask the Holy Spirit to guide you into truth. He is the only one who can do this anyway. When I give a scripture reference, have your Bible handy and look up the scriptures for yourself. Just think, every time you read a scripture you are engaging in dialogue with Jesus. He is the word!

GOD'S PART

CHAPTER 1

GOD'S PART: HIS LOVE

We have the Bible to teach us who God is, but how many of us really know him? How many of us really know what God's part is in this thing called life? Do we judge his character and nature based on our experiences or the experiences of others?

In God's sovereignty, he has given us the written word to learn about him, and to reveal to us what is available for us through his son, Jesus Christ, who is the word (John 1:14). As we begin our research about who God is, let's go directly to the source.

In the Bible, it tells us that *"**all** scripture is given by inspiration of God, and is profitable for doctrine, for reproof, for correction, and for instruction in righteousness..."* (2 Timothy 3:16 emphasis added). Now, you have to decide whether you believe what you just read is absolute truth revealed by God himself, through the Holy Spirit.

As you read the pages of this book, I encourage you to get your Bible and read the scripture references for yourself. Only the Holy Spirit can guide you into truth (John 16:13). Jesus said, *"if you continue in my word, then are ye my disciples indeed; and ye shall know the truth, and the truth shall make you free"* (John 8:31-32). Before reading further, you must decide on two things: are you earnestly seeking to know truth, and will you choose to believe what you find based on the written word of God? Then, what will you do with the truth that you learn?

Let's journey through some of God's word that reveals who he is, and what he has done for us. This is only a glimpse into the word and is by no means all-inclusive. My prayer is that this will stir you up to pursue God through his word in the Bible on your own.

God is Love

Don't you just want to know more about God's love for you? It is his nature, who he is, and what he has done to demonstrate his love for us. Jesus himself said, *"For God so **loved the world**, that **he gave his only begotten Son**, that whosoever believeth in him should not perish, but have everlasting life. For God sent not his Son into the world to condemn the world; but that the world through him might be saved"* (John 3:16-17 emphasis added).

The word "saved" in the Greek translation of the Bible is defined as "to save, i.e. deliver or protect, heal, preserve, save, do well, be (make) whole." So, not only do we learn in these scriptures that God loved the whole world that he gave his Son for our eternal destination, but because he isn't in the business of condemning us, his Son made a way for us to have a whole, healthy, prosperous life while we are in this world.

Check out Isaiah 53:4-5 and read about the prophecy of Jesus, and all that he would endure for man's sake. *"Surely he hath borne our griefs, and carried our sorrows: yet we did esteem him stricken, smitten of God, and afflicted. But he was wounded for our transgressions, he was bruised for our iniquities: the chastisement of our peace was upon him; and with his stripes we are healed."*

I love how God has laid out his word. You are able to see how his word was spoken, and then later, you see his spoken word fulfilled. God has preserved the word for us to show that he cannot lie (Titus 1:2).

Read Matthew 8:14-17. Jesus healed and delivered the sick, and those possessed with devils that it would be fulfilled based on what the prophet Isaiah had spoken. Look at what Peter says happened after the crucifixion of Jesus: *"who his own self bare our sins in his own body on the tree, that we, being dead to sins, should live unto righteousness: by whose stripes ye were healed"* (1 Peter 2:24). Here are examples of three different written accounts of God's love providing for our eternal destination, our wholeness, and for health in our physical bodies through his spoken word, and the fulfillment through the beating of Jesus.

Paul says it this way, *"For by grace through faith you are **saved**..."* (Ephesians 2:8 emphasis added). Remember our Greek definition of the word saved from earlier? God's demonstration of his love for mankind was fulfilled through Jesus Christ.

When you heard the word about Jesus Christ, believed it in your heart, and confessed it with your mouth, the Bible says that you were saved (Romans 10:9). God then sent forth the Spirit of his Son into your heart (Galatians 4:6) and sealed you until the day of redemption (Ephesians 4:30). Now, the Holy Spirit is able to reveal to your heart the love of God (Romans 5:5). The Holy Spirit is now your Comforter, who teaches you all things, and brings things back to your remembrance (John 14:26). He has been given to you to help you know the deep things of God, and to know the things that have been freely given to you by God (1 Corinthians 2:10).

When we accept the free gift of righteousness, and embrace the finished work of the cross, we participate in God's kingdom as joint heirs with Christ. That is why we can give thanks to the Father, *"which hath made us meet to be partakers of the inheritance of the saints in light: Who hath delivered us from the power of darkness, and **hath translated us into the kingdom of his dear Son**: In whom we have redemption through his blood, even the forgiveness of sins* (Colossians 1:12-14 emphasis added). This is another example of what God has done for us. We are in his kingdom NOW. Does this look and sound like something familiar? Can we go back to Genesis when God created everything, and on day six created man? Everything had been done for man by God, and then God rested because he had finished what needed to be done. Disobedience to God took place; sin entered; their relationship was severed, and man lost his place of rest.

But now, we see *"that God was in Christ, reconciling the world unto himself, not imputing their trespasses unto them; and hath committed unto us the word of reconciliation"* (2 Corinthians 5:19). Through Christ, we are in his kingdom, his domain. We now have access to the throne of grace! We can go boldly to obtain mercy, and find grace to help in time of need (Hebrews 4:16)! Whatever we have need of from our Father, it is yes and amen (2 Corinthians 1:20).

Stop right now! Ask the Holy Spirit to help you know the love of God. The Holy Spirit was given to you to gush into your heart the love of your Heavenly Father. Are you getting a picture of how much God loves you? The words of life through the scriptures should be resonating throughout your entire being.

CHAPTER 2

GOD'S PART: IT IS FINISHED

One of my favorite sayings of my husband, Harold, is, "Keep it simple." Isn't that what Jesus did? He taught with word pictures. He gave illustrations that a farmer could understand. I can relate, not because of my IQ level or intellectual knowledge, but because I have the Holy Spirit.

As I read my Father's word through the guidance of the Holy Spirit, there are things that just seem to be so clear, yet so many miss the simplicity of the gospel of grace. This isn't to diminish the importance or severity of what took place, however as a disciple of Jesus Christ, an ambassador, a good soldier, and all of the other positions that he has placed me in, he did it all. It is finished.

This is how simple it is to me:

- God Almighty spoke everything into existence.
- He created mankind for fellowship with him.
- Man disobeyed God and sin entered the world.
- Sin wreaked havoc in the earth.

- God so loved the world that he sent his Son to redeem man so that he could have fellowship with man again.

- Jesus Christ took all authority away from Satan, yet Satan still has ability to the degree that we are deceived by his lies.

- When we received the free gift of salvation by believing that God raised Jesus on the third day and we confessed him as Lord and Savior, he gave us his Spirit and born us again, spiritually. When he moved in, we received the fruit, the gifts, and the power of the Spirit.

- We were placed in his kingdom.

- He gave us his armor.

- He gave us his word.

- He made us sons, ambassadors, soldiers, kings, and priests.

- Now we have a responsibility to advance and increase his kingdom on the earth by letting our *"light so shine before men, that they may see your good works, and glorify your Father which is in heaven"* (Matthew 5:16). When light invades darkness, captives are set free. We are here to invade territories of darkness with the light of Jesus Christ.

- We are to encourage the lost with demonstration of the Holy Spirit and power in order to reveal the Father's love and show them how to come home.

In God's sovereignty, he chose to place the spiritual and natural laws in order by his spoken word. Our role is to believe what he has already spoken and perform it the way he designed it. We must stop trying to explain away things like why God's word doesn't work, why it is not applicable in this dispensation, and whatever other rhetoric is out there regarding what God said in his word. Humility and submission is required in order to walk in the grace and kingdom that has been provided through Jesus Christ. It is so good when we totally surrender, trust, and obey. There are no second acts and God is no respecter of persons (Acts 10:34). If he'll do it for me and he'll do it for others, he'll do it for you. Believing his word and acting on his word is an incredible journey!

SATAN'S PART

CHAPTER 3

SATAN'S PART: FATHER OF LIES

L et me start out this section by saying what Jesus said in Matthew 28:18: *"And Jesus came and spake unto them, saying, **All** power is given unto me in heaven and in earth."* (emphasis added) Look how Paul describes it in Colossians 2:14-15:

> *"Blotting out the handwriting of ordinances that was against us, which was contrary to us, and took it out of the way, nailing it to his cross; and having spoiled principalities and powers, **he made a shew of them openly, triumphing over them in it."** (emphasis added)*

Isn't that a great picture of victory? In order for there to be a victory, there had to be a battle. A war of some sort. If there are still captives in bondage to darkness, who is their enemy? I'm going to list a few of the descriptions of our enemy so you are not deceived or blinded to who is after your destruction:

- A thief that comes to steal, kill, and destroy. (John 10:10)
- A murderer with no truth in him, who speaks lies. (John 8:44)
- A liar and the father of lies. (John 8:44)
- Accuser of the brethren. (Revelation 12:10)
- Our adversary who wants to devour us. (1 Peter 5:8)
- He has devices to try and get an advantage over us. (2 Corinthians 2:11)
- He uses fiery darts of deception. (Ephesians 6:16)
- There are levels of his dominion of darkness. (Ephesians 6:12)
- He can be transformed into an angel of light. (2 Corinthians 11:14)

Based on these scriptures alone, how can anyone compare God's sovereignty with the works of the devil? When someone, in their ignorance to God's love and word, accuses him of allowing or doing something that steals, kills, or destroys one of his own children, it is preposterous. One cannot look at Jesus Christ, the cross, his stripes, his shed blood, his resurrection, and his giving of his Spirit to a believer, and come to that conclusion under the guidance of the Holy Spirit. Please do not get into condemnation if you have been guilty of this. Tell him you are sorry, get the truth in you and be transformed by the renewing of your mind (Romans 12:2).

TESTIMONY OF APPLYING GOD'S WORD

I think we all have grown up knowing that there is a devil, along with the various descriptions of what he is and how he looks. Until I began to read the word of God, I had no idea at the level of my ignorance. I would cry out to God asking him why things kept happening to me, and yet I kept sowing to my flesh. When you sow to your flesh, from your flesh you reap corruption (Galatians 6:7-8). I continued to empower the enemy in my life due to my own ignorance of who he was, but more importantly, of who I was in Christ.

At the prompting of the Holy Spirit, I am going to share a testimony that involves my mother. For the first time in my adult life, I feel the desire and overwhelming need to protect and honor my mother. In the power of forgiveness, and the revelation of the enemy's tactics to steal, kill, and destroy, I see my relationship with her and my less-than-perfect upbringing so differently now. It is no longer the blame game or about shedding darkness, but rather sharing truth in love. That is my hope for you as I share one of the ploys that the enemy used against my life and against my family.

I left home when I was a junior in high school. Amazing families took me in, including one of my teachers and her husband. When I was in college, God brought another woman into my life who has been like a mother to me all of these years.

As life rolled by, I saw my mom twice in a twenty-five-year span. My parents were divorced and I maintained a relationship with my daddy. My parents were raised in church, but my siblings and I were not. My mom did teach us who Jesus was though.

As the Lord began to deal with my heart regarding forgiveness, I knew I had to contact her. I made the call and asked her to forgive me for judging her. I came to understand that the enemy had been trying to destroy her and all that she had, including our relationship.

One day I received a call from Adult Protection Services in Texas informing me that if I didn't come and do something with my mother that they were going to have her committed to a facility of their choosing. So, my husband, Harold, and I went to my mom's home in Texas. I didn't even recognize her. It was heart wrenching to say the least. However, my seven-year-old son crawled right up on the couch with her and introduced himself.

Over this two-year period, we were able to get her into a nursing home that was half way between my sister, who lives in Texas, and us in Louisiana. My son and I would go every Thursday to visit her. She had not changed, but I did. I would buy her candy and cigarettes every week along with the other requests she made.

One day the Lord asked me why I was contributing to that destructive spirit by buying her cigarettes. (Now those of you who smoke, don't allow the spirit of offense to come on you! I'm just telling you what the Lord spoke to me about my mom.) When I showed up with no cigarettes, you can imagine my mother's loud and colorful language. I felt like I was twelve again as that spirit on her began to yell at me in front of my son. I asked him to leave the room. I calmly yet sternly told her that she would not yell at me again, and especially not in front of my son. She responded by saying she wasn't up to having us visit. That was my cue to leave, and I was happy to oblige her request.

My son began to ask me why I let her yell at me that way. I reminded him that our struggle is not with flesh and blood. However, in my mind, all it did was take me back to the fact that she was still the same.

Later that night, I told the Lord that I was not going back to visit her. I lived my whole adult life without her, and I was doing just fine. Do you know how the Lord responded? He gently asked me, "Are you going to continue to allow the enemy to steal from you?"

What! The scripture about stealing, killing, and destroying jolted me back into reality (John 10:10). I then meditated on the second part of those words that Jesus spoke saying he came to give me life and life more abundantly. I decided from then on, I would walk in love, light, and command those spirits to leave my mother.

You see, the enemy had destroyed her with lies of shame and guilt. I now saw that. For two years, God gave me the grace to love my mother, and to teach her of his love and forgiveness. It wasn't always easy, but his grace was sufficient. The last time I saw her, my sister and I recited Psalms 23 over her. My mother taught us Psalms 23 when we were children. There were times she would even make us write it out as a form of punishment.

More than three decades later, as my sister and I prayed God's word over our dying mother tears welled up in both our souls. *"The Lord is my shepherd; I shall not want. He maketh me to lie down in green pastures: he leadeth me beside the still waters. He restoreth my soul: he leadeth me in the paths of righteousness for his name's sake. Yea, though I walk through the valley of the shadow of death, I will fear no evil: for thou art with me; thy rod and thy staff they comfort me. Thou preparest a table before me in the presence of mine enemies: thou anointest my head with oil; my cup runneth over. Surely goodness and mercy shall follow me all the days of my life: and I will dwell in the house of the Lord for ever."*

It warmed both our hearts to know our mom was able to witness this harvest during her lifetime, a harvest of love, grace, mercy and forgiveness from the seeds (God's word) that she planted in us as young girls oh so many years before. My sister and I both were so thankful that God gave us that special day with her before she went to be with Jesus. I almost allowed the enemy to steal the two years of restoration that God was trying to give us. I'm so grateful for the Holy Spirit and the word of God directing our hearts in this area of forgiveness. Three hearts were forever restored that day.

APPLICATION ASSIGNMENT

1. Ask the Holy Spirit to reveal one area of your life that the enemy is stealing from you.

2. Read John 10:10 and James 4:7.

3. Ask the Holy Spirit for revelation.

4. Speak those scriptures out loud. Romans 10:17 says, *"Faith cometh by hearing, and hearing by the word of God."*

5. Stand your ground with the word of God and declare to the enemy that he will steal from you no more.

6. Journal your journey.

YOUR PART

CHAPTER 4

YOUR PART: WHAT HAPPENS WHEN YOU ARE BORN AGAIN?

I like most Christians, had no biblical understanding of what happened , the moment I received the gift of salvation. I'm not going to say I fully comprehend everything that was included in the free gift of righteousness, however in my simple childlike faith, I will share what Jesus has taught me through experience, and the word. I give honor to the men, women, and children I have listened to, read about, and/or have learned from over the years regarding their knowledge of Jesus Christ. I love this journey of drawing near to God as he draws near to me (James 4:8). I'll share with you some of what I have learned in my pursuit of Jesus, my Lord. Let's first look at a few scriptures on how God sees you:

> *Before I formed you in the womb I knew and approved of you...* (Jeremiah 1:5 AMP)

> *For I know the thoughts that I think toward you, saith the Lord, thoughts of peace, and not of evil, to give you an expected end.* (Jeremiah 29:11)

Thou art worthy, O Lord, to receive glory and honour and power: for thou hast created all things, and for thy pleasure they are and were created. (Revelation 4:11)

How precious also are thy thoughts unto me, O God! how great is the sum of them! If I should count them, they are more in number than the sand: when I awake, I am still with thee. (Psalms 139:17-18)

So, what do these scriptures say to you? Here's what they say to me and my heart: God knew me before I was conceived; his thoughts of me are "shalom." This is the Hebrew word that means *"well, happy, friendly, health, prosperity, and peace"* (NSECB). He has a hopeful future for me; he created me for his pleasure; and his thoughts of me are more in number than all of the grains of sand! His word says these things about you as well. He is no respecter of persons according to Acts 10:34.

One of the jobs of the Holy Spirit is to reveal to your heart that God loves you.

And hope maketh not ashamed; because the love of God is shed abroad in our hearts by the Holy Ghost which is given unto us (Romans 5:5).

Now with some scriptures under your belt about how God sees you, let's look at some of the things that happened the moment you accepted the free gift of salvation and the Holy Spirit moved in. Paul reveals to us in 1 Thessalonians 5:23 that we are a spirit, we have a soul, and are encased in a physical body. I have heard many teach that when you are saved, old things have passed away, and all things have become new. How could that be taught when I still looked the same, talked the same, acted the same, and thought the same? Let's read the scripture that I am referring to, including the one before it:

Wherefore henceforth know we no man after the flesh: yea, though we have known Christ after the flesh, yet now henceforth know we him no more. Therefore if any man be in Christ, he is a new creature: old things are passed away; behold, all things have become new. (2 Corinthians 5:16-17)

Paul is saying that we are not to know man or Jesus in the flesh, so how are we to see or know people? How is a man "in Christ"? What did Jesus say about this?

> But the hour cometh, and now is, when the true worshippers shall worship the Father in spirit and in truth: for the Father seeketh such to worship him. God is a Spirit: and they that worship him must worship him in spirit and in truth. (John 4:23-24)

We are to know one another by the Spirit. Our spirit is what was born again. This part of us is where old things passed away, and all things became new. This truth was such a revelation to me. It set me free from condemnation in areas of constant failure. Our physical body did not change or Paul would not have told us in Romans 12:1 to present our bodies a living sacrifice. Our mind did not change, or Paul would not have told us in Romans 12:2 to renew our mind that so we could prove God's acceptable, perfect will. Look at the following scripture:

> In whom ye also trusted, after that ye heard the word of truth, the gospel of your salvation: in whom also after that ye believed, ye were **sealed** with that holy Spirit of promise, which is the earnest of our inheritance until the redemption of the purchased possession, unto the praise of his glory. (Ephesians 1:13-14 emphasis added)

You were sealed with the Holy Spirit in your spirit. The best illustration that I can visualize is when I make preserves. Once the fruit has been cleaned, chopped, cooked, jars are sterilized and water bath is boiling, you can add the filled jars to the hot water. At the appointed time, the jars are pulled from the water and set on the counter for the lids to seal. Anyone who cans knows that sound. The jars are sealed and nothing is getting inside that sealed jar!

Paul has so many scriptures revealing what happened in this miracle of being born again. Read all of Paul's epistles (his letters to the churches) from this revelation of being new in your spirit. I'll list a few here to show you this truth:

> But he that is joined unto the Lord is **one spirit**. (1 Corinthians 6:17 emphasis added)

I am crucified with Christ: nevertheless I live; yet not I, but **Christ liveth in me**: *and the life which I now live in the flesh I live by the faith of the Son of God, who loved me, and gave himself for me.* (Galatians 2:20 emphasis added)

For ye are all the children of God by faith in Christ Jesus. For as many of you as have been baptized into Christ have put on Christ. There is neither Jew nor Greek, there is neither bond nor free, there is neither male nor female: for ye are all one in Christ Jesus. And if ye be Christ's, then are ye Abraham's seed, and heirs according to the promise. (Galatians 3:26-29)

Herein is our love made perfect, that we may have boldness in the day of judgment: because as he is, so are we in this world. (1 John 4:17)

For God hath not given us the spirit of fear; but of power, and of love, and of a sound mind. (2 Timothy 1:7)

I had a conversation with my pawpaw (my grandfather on my father's side) several years before he went to be with Jesus. He knew the Old Testament very well, and I loved to hear him tell Bible stories around the dinner table when I was a little girl.

Around twelve years ago, as I began to read the Bible for myself, I was excited that I would finally be able to carry on an intelligent conversation with him in this area. My husband, Harold, told me to read Paul's teachings first, because Paul's revelation was what took place after the cross. He reminded me that what's contained in Paul's epistles are who we are today.

In my conversation with my pawpaw, I began to talk about Paul and his writings. I shared the revelation about the born-again spirit, and specifically, Galatians 3:26-29. He was not as excited about this as I was. He said to me that he was a male and I was a female, so how could we all be one in Christ Jesus. I shared that it was in the spirit part of us. He told me that even theologians said that Paul's writings were too hard to comprehend, and that he didn't understand them. I was discerning that he did not want to discuss this any longer. I then asked for help from the Holy Spirit to guide me in our conversation. We talked about King David and a few others from the Old Testament, which was much more agreeable with him. I began to see clearer the importance of the role of the Holy Spirit giving me revelation as I read the word, and what Jesus meant when he said that the word is "spirit and life" (John 6:63). Only the Holy Spirit can guide you into truth (John 16:13). Look what Jesus said:

> *It is the spirit that quickeneth; the flesh profiteth nothing:*
> *the words that I speak unto you, they are **spirit**, and they*
> *are **life**.* (John 6:63 emphasis added)

We cannot comprehend God with our carnal mind. It is in opposition to God (Romans 8:6-7). Why do you think that there are so many Bible translations? People are trying to intellectualize God's word and make it understandable to their carnal mind. All we have to do is humble ourselves and ask the Holy Spirit for the spirit of wisdom and revelation in the knowledge of him (Ephesians 1:17). He promises that when we ask, it will be given to us; seek, and we will find; knock, and the door is opened (Matthew 7:7).

TESTIMONY OF APPLYING GOD'S WORD

Here's a personal testimony of how I applied the word in my life and became a doer of the word. If we do not do the word, we deceive ourselves.

> *But be ye doers of the word, and not hearers only, deceiving*
> *your own selves.* (James 1:22)

Let me first share how this "doing the word" began in my pursuit of knowing God. As far back as I can remember, I have always known Jesus and have had conversations with him. However, I did not know him based on his word. I was like many others who knew God could do anything because he was God. Even when things were chaotic in my life, and I saw the chaos in others' lives, I never had the tendency to blame God. When my fifteen-year-old sister died in a car accident, many said that God needed another angel in heaven. Are you kidding me? First of all, we are not angels. Second of all, I didn't believe that God "took her." Even in my ignorance of his word, I knew that my Jesus was good!

With my filter being that God was and is good, my heart was able to receive the amazing promises with childlike faith. Now, walking it out wasn't always easy. It is still what Paul refers to as the *"good fight of faith"* (1 Timothy 6:12).

When my son was four months old, our pediatrician told us he had a heart murmur. The doctor referred us to a pediatric cardiologist who diagnosed him with supravalvular aortic stenosis. The same day we received the diagnosis and were told that he would eventually have to have surgery, we were told that this diagnosis is one of the characteristic findings in children with Williams syndrome. This is a genetic disorder that has various complications, including intellectual disabilities, a face that has "elfin" features, and a shorter life expectancy.

As I looked at this perfectly healthy looking baby, I could not comprehend what I was hearing in the matter of a two-hour office visit. We were referred to a genetic doctor for the testing to confirm or deny the Williams syndrome suspicion. In the weeks that followed, the testing revealed that he did not have Williams syndrome.

We wanted a second opinion regarding the heart diagnosis, so we ended up going to Texas Children's Hospital in Houston. The diagnosis of aortic stenosis was confirmed. The doctor told us that a stent would not work because of where the crimp was located. The surgery would involve sectioning out the crimped area of the aorta. All this talk of surgery had my head spinning, but the doctor assured us that surgery was not necessary just yet because "there was a one in a million chance my son would a have heart attack." What! Yes, that is what we were told as a way of reassuring us that we should go home and treat our son like a normal baby. The doctor added that he would have his surgical team monitor my son, and when they felt it was time for surgery, they'd call us to get our affairs in order.

What I didn't know in the beginning of this baby journey was that a friend of ours, Rebecca, was praying for me the entire time. When my son was diagnosed, she asked to come and pray for him. She held him and talked to him. She wasn't begging God to heal him. She was speaking to his heart and was coming into agreement with what God had already said in his word about healing. She was so sweet and confident. Another couple came and anointed him with oil and prayed over him.

The next trip to Houston, the doctor told us that because of the scar tissue building up on his valve, they would have to do a valve replacement in addition to the sectioning of the aorta. Rebecca was not moved by this news. She came again and spoke to his heart.

Many things were going on in my life during this time. I was just trying to survive one day at a time, so I simply would not entertain thoughts of heart surgery. In my ignorance of God's will according to his word, the enemy was destroying every area of my life. I was not aware of all that Jesus had accomplished for me when he was beaten, crucified, raised from the dead, and then sent his Spirit into me on the day I was born again. I did not know that I was in a spiritual battle with an enemy that I could not see but had dominion over because of Jesus Christ. Oh, I could recite the Lord's prayer because we prayed it in school. I knew John 3:16 because I heard it over and over again as others said it.

The night before I was to take my son back to Houston for another checkup, I read the Bible story of Abraham and Isaac for the first time. In my ignorance to God's will regarding healing, but with childlike faith, I told the Lord that if Abraham could give Isaac back to him then I could too. I got on my knees beside my son's toddler bed sobbing, and gave him back to the Lord. I asked the Lord for strength and courage regardless of the outcome.

When my friend picked me up the next morning to drive us to Houston, I asked her, "Have you ever left your house knowing that when you returned, your life would be forever changed?" Boy, was I about to find out the meaning of that statement! There was a war going on in my mind and heart. My mind was trying to prepare for more bad news, but my heart had a sense of unexplainable peace.

After my son recovered from the anesthesia, the doctor came in and was very quiet. He had spent more time than usual listening to my son's heart and reviewing the tests results. He rolled back on his stool and looked at us. "I don't know how to say this," he began, "but I have never been able to tell parents this news with this kind of heart condition. Not only has he not gotten worse or stayed the same, but he has improved. I can't explain it."

My friend Kay, who was accompanying me, cried. My son's dad, who was there too, cried. I, instead, grinned from ear to ear. I said, "I can explain it. It's an answer to prayer!" The doctor agreed with me.

As I sat in the lobby of Texas Children's Hospital waiting for our truck to be brought to the front, I thanked God. However, my heart was asking him why my baby. What about these other babies? This is where my journey in his word began. I had to know more about this God that I said I trusted for my eternal salvation yet knew nothing more than the surface stuff about my sins being forgiven, and that I was going to heaven. Sound familiar?

After leaving the hospital, you know the first person I called? Yep, my friend Rebecca! She was not surprised at the amazing news. She rejoiced with me knowing it was an answer to prayer.

Within two years, another friend who God brought into my life, Rhonda, introduced me to Andrew Wommack and his ministry and teachings. She knew that I did not know who I was in Christ, nor did I understand all that God accomplished through Jesus. Another chapter was beginning in my life as I pursued my Father through his word.

After being exposed to truth regarding my identity in Christ, I had to come to terms that I had a responsibility to the gospel. With responsibility comes accountability and most do not want it. How could I look at what Jesus said, "...*freely ye have received, freely give*" (Matthew 10:8), and ignore it? What could I do with what Jesus said when he told those who believe to speak to the mountain?

> "*And Jesus answering saith unto them, Have faith in God.*
> *For verily I say unto you, That whosoever shall say unto*
> *this mountain, Be thou removed, and be thou cast into*
> *the sea; and shall not doubt in his heart, but shall believe*
> *that those things which he saith shall come to pass; he*
> *shall have whatsoever he saith. Therefore I say unto you,*
> *What things soever ye desire, when ye pray, believe that*
> *ye receive them, and ye shall have them.*" (Mark 11:22-24)

When I heard and saw this truth, the Holy Spirit brought back to me how Rebecca spoke to my son's body. I called her and asked if she had heard of

Andrew Wommack and she told me that she watched him on TV every day. I then shared my revelation that I believed she spoke to my son's heart based on Mark 11. She agreed saying that she did. Excitement building in my soul at the truth unfolding before me, I then stated, "You believed that you received when you prayed!" With a calming sweetness in her voice, she affirmed that this is the way she indeed prayed over my son's heart.

Approximately thirteen years ago God's word manifested in my son's body because of Rebecca's act of obedience and faith in the promise of the seed regarding healing. Remember, the seed is God's word. I remind her occasionally of the fruit and rewards that are going to her account in heaven (1 Corinthians 3:13-14). Everything that my family does now for the advancement of God's kingdom goes to her account—and my friend Rhonda's account—because of their faith in God's word, and obedience to do the word. These women didn't just hear the word and mentally agree. Faith manifested as they stepped out to do what they believed based on the word of God.

Faith has risen up in me just by sharing this testimony that happened more than a decade ago. Let's look at what John wrote in Revelation 12:10-11 regarding the word of our testimony:

> "And I heard a loud voice saying in heaven, Now is come salvation, and strength, and the kingdom of our God, and the power of his Christ: for the accuser of our brethren is cast down, which accused them before our God day and night. And they overcame him by the blood of the Lamb, and by the **word of their testimony**; and they loved not their lives unto the death." (Revelation 12:10-11, emphasis added)

There is so much in these scriptures, but I want to draw your attention to the part where it says the accuser (Satan) was overcome by the blood of Jesus and when we put word to our testimony. So, share what Jesus has done in your life!

After returning to Texas Children's Hospital for one last time, the doctor saw no reason for us to return. When my son turned eleven, he wanted to join the Navy League Cadet Corps. The Navy requires a complete physical each year in order for him to continue in the program. The second pediatrician that we started going to when he was three was the doctor completing the physicals. We were able to share the healing testimony with him and, most recently, with his son who took over his practice when he retired. They both said that they believed in miracles.

Before knowing the previous referenced scripture, Revelation 12:10-11, I went back to the two churches that I had been attending during the two-year battle and shared the testimony. The first church was silent and didn't know how to respond. The second church was not as awkward, but the pastor did comment that it was a miracle. I had many tell me that the doctors made a mistake. As a believer seeking truth based on God's word, it was beyond my simple childlike faith to comprehend how other Christians could not just simply believe what God has said.

As you read the testimonies that I share, all based on God's word, you have a choice to make. You can choose to ask for revelation for yourself, or you can choose not to believe. God's love for you does not change. If you don't believe, then God's word won't work for you. Oh, but the joy you have when you do believe!

> *"Whom having not seen, ye love; in whom, though now ye see him not, yet **believing, ye rejoice with joy unspeakable and full of glory...**"* (1 Peter 1:8 emphasis added)

APPLICATION ASSIGNMENT

1. For you not to be deceived, I am going to give you an opportunity to apply what has been shared in this section. Get your Bible and journal. Ask the Holy Spirit for wisdom and revelation (Ephesians 1:17) because he is your guide into truth (John 16:13).

2. Read Galatians 2:20 out loud. Think about it and write it down where you can see it several times a day. Sow it in your heart. Continually ask the Holy Spirit to reveal truth to you about you and Christ.

3. Write down the things that he reveals to you about Galatians 2:20. I have worked on one scripture for many weeks before moving to another. Remember, Jesus is the word! (John 1:1, John 1:14)

CHAPTER 5

YOUR PART: WHAT DID THE HOLY SPIRIT BRING WHEN HE MOVED IN TO YOUR TEMPLE?

When I had trouble conceiving my son, I was referred to a fertility specialist. I was thirty-six years old before I began to grasp any sort of understanding of the complexity of all that is involved in the female body when it comes to conception. I knew the basics like anyone else until the process of elimination started on why I was not getting pregnant. What a miracle the human body is in its intricate workings. God is so amazing! As an educated person, I felt totally ignorant to the body that I had been carrying around for thirty-six years.

Guess what? When I learned that the Holy Spirit moved in to my temple, this body, I was not going to let ignorance rule my life again! Look at how Jesus described the Holy Spirit in John 14:16-17: *"And I will pray the Father, and he shall give you another **Comforter**, that he may abide with you for ever; Even the **Spirit of truth**; whom the world cannot receive, because it seeth him not, neither knoweth him: but ye know him; for he dwelleth with you, and shall **be in you**."* (emphasis added)

What is the role of the Holy Spirit in the life of a believer according to Jesus?

> *But the **Comforter**, which is the Holy Ghost, whom the*
> *Father will send in my name, he shall **teach you all things**,*
> *and **bring all things to your remembrance**, whatsoever*
> *I have said unto you.* (John 14:26 emphasis added)

Oh my! Do you see this? The Holy Spirit's role is to teach you ALL things, and then he is going to bring it back to your memory. If I had a nickel for every person who told me that they can't remember scripture, I would have a large sum! That statement is contrary to what Jesus said about the responsibility of the Holy Spirit in your life.

I experienced the reality of this one day several years ago. I was ministering in a nursing home to two women in a room. One of the ladies would ramble and "talk out of her head." There would be moments of clarity for her, but most of the time, it was just rambling. When I would begin to pray and quote scriptures, she would raise her hands and quote them with me. I would watch as her entire countenance changed and peace would come. I knew that it was the Holy Spirit bringing the scriptures back to her memory. It was fascinating to me as I grew in the word, knowing that Jesus is the word (John 1:1, John 1:14). The Holy Spirit will guide you into all truth and show you things to come.

> *Howbeit when he, the Spirit of truth, is come, he will guide*
> *you into all truth: for he shall not speak of himself; but*
> *whatsoever he shall hear, that shall he speak: and he will*
> ***shew you things to come***. (John 16:13 emphasis added)

Are you getting the idea of who is inside of you as a believer? What is truth? God's word. This is why Paul's prayer for us in Ephesians 1:18-19 is that we would be enlightened to the power that is on the inside of us. It is Christ in us, the hope of glory (Colossians 1:27).

What else does the Holy Spirit do in our lives? He makes known in our hearts how much God loves us (Romans 5:5). He reveals the things that God has given to us that love him (1 Corinthians 2:9). He searches the deep things of God to reveal the things that he has freely given to us (1 Corinthians 2:10, 12). He makes intercession for us, and prays the perfect will of God when we don't know what or how to pray (Romans 8:26-27).

Have you spent time in the word learning who the Holy Spirit is? Have you recognized his presence in your everyday life? Do you see how invaluable this relationship is just on these few scriptures? This is by no means an all-inclusive list of scriptures. I just wanted to show you a few that have resonated so much with me. The acknowledgment of him and his presence, based on the word, has changed my life.

What are the Holy Spirit's characteristics? What is his nature? How do you know if he is leading you, or your flesh is leading you? Paul describes him in Galatians 5:22 as love, joy, peace, longsuffering, gentleness, goodness, faith, meekness, and temperance. Anytime you are responding with these attributes, you are being led by the Holy Spirit. Read Galatians 5:19-21 for the works of the flesh. When you are led by these, the results are found in Galatians 6:7-8.

As a believer, would you agree that God has given you gifts, a calling specific to you? A purpose? If your answer is yes, what scripture(s) come to mind? If no, what is your reason based on the word of God? I'll show you just a few scriptures and let the Holy Spirit reveal truth:

> *For the gifts and calling of God are without repentance.*
> (Romans 11:29)

> *Even as the testimony of Christ was confirmed in you: so that ye come behind in no gift; waiting for the coming of our Lord Jesus Christ.* (1 Corinthians 1:6-7)

> *For I know the plans and thoughts that I have for you, says the LORD, plans for peace and well-being and not for disaster to give you a future and a hope.*
> (Jeremiah 29:11 AMP)

Will you agree that the Holy Spirit is a "he" and not an "it"? Did Jesus refer to the Holy Spirit as "he"? Yes, he did. Go back and read John 14:16-17. When he moved in, did you only receive a portion of him? Did the Father hold out on you? If you have gifts given to you (Romans 11:29, James 1:17), don't you think the Holy Spirit has gifts also? If he took up residence in your physical body, what did he not bring with him regarding his fruit and his gifts?

Before I move on, ask the Holy Spirit for guidance and revelation into these truths. You have not because you ask not, so ask (Matthew 7:7, James 4:2).

Paul tells us that there are diversities of gifts, differences of administrations, and diversities of operations, but that they are all by the same Spirit (1 Corinthians 12:4-7). They are all by the Holy Spirit who is in you, who is the same Holy Spirit that is in me, and in every other person who is a believer in Jesus Christ. This is the same Holy Spirit who was in Jesus when he was raised from the dead (Ephesians 1:17-20).

I experienced a revelation of this truth and the reality of it when I went on a mission trip to Haiti in 2014. The day I received this revelation, our mission team and I were scheduled to go to the Saint Marc prison, but when we arrived the leadership of the prison would not let us enter. For our day to not be wasted, the mission team leaders drove us to a village and said that they would proceed with setting up for medical missions.

Before we got off the bus, the leaders explained to the crowd of 350 villagers that if anyone needed prayer to look for someone wearing a blue shirt. There were twenty-four of us on the mission team wearing blue shirts. It was important we stood out in such a large crowd.

We also had one translator for every two people on the team. As I looked out the windows of the bus, doubt began to flood my thoughts. For a split second, I felt inadequate, ill equipped, and powerless. Who was I? Just a girl from the country who had some education and knew a few scriptures looking over a crowd of people who came for help and answers. I told the Holy Spirit as I descended the stairs of the bus, "I have nothing to offer them. I'll do my part, but I need you to do your part." He was bringing back to my remembrance who I was in Christ. This is another reason that I always recommend that we sow Galatians 2:20 in our hearts. It is such a powerful, applicable, mind-renewing scripture to who lives in us.

The crowd pressed in on the mission team for prayer. Fortunately, I was separated with a translator. However, the spirit of fear crept up on me as the many hands from the locals began reaching and touching my body completely engulfing me with their presence. I asked the translator to give me just a minute. I closed my eyes and commanded fear to leave me. As fear left, I had an overwhelming sense of peace. I then began to feel something that was familiar, like I had been in this position before. (By the way, this was my first time to Haiti, and my first mission trip.) With eyes closed, I asked the Holy Spirit to tell me what this sensation was. He responded, "I am the same Spirit that was with Jesus when he ministered to the multitudes."

I don't know how to explain this in words other than it was one of those "aha" moments. Know what I am talking about? It's when revelation moves from our born-again spirit into our soul! Light explodes on the inside. The scripture in Ephesians erupted into reality in my innermost being.

I opened my eyes with a sense of unending peace, courage, and boldness. I saw the one standing in front of me, not seeing all of the others in my "space" waiting for prayer. I told my translator that I was ready to minister. As the moments ticked by, someone tapped me on the shoulder and told me it was time for a water break. I had been praying for more than three hours and never got thirsty or tired.

It reminded me of what Jesus said, *"But whosoever drinketh of the water that I shall give him shall never thirst; but the water that I shall give him shall be in him a well of water springing up into everlasting life"* (John 4:14). And yes, I know we need physical drinking water! This is a spiritual principle I experienced through revelation of the Holy Spirit as I did the word.

I also have a better understanding of why Jesus began his explanation of Mark 4:13 that if you didn't understand this parable, you wouldn't understand the rest of what he taught in parables. It is the word in our hearts that produces the fruit of the promise in our lives. The Holy Spirit brought back to my remembrance the word when my thoughts and feelings were acting contrary to the word, based on what I was seeing with my eyes in the natural. He never told us to build our house on our emotions. They are ever changing! Sometimes they change minute to minute depending on who says what to you. Would you agree? Our foundation must be the word of God.

Do you see how the word works? It is just words on a page in a book on a table until you pick it up. You read it; you sow the word (seed) in your heart; you let the Holy Spirit guide you into the truth and revelation of that word (seed); and then you are able to experience the life that is in that word (seed), i.e. the fruit of it (Mark 4:11-20).

The Holy Spirit is who our Father has sent to live in you, to help you understand the principles that he, in his sovereignty, has established in his kingdom. This is who moved in to your temple when you accepted Jesus as your Lord and Savior. Why don't you go ahead and reintroduce yourself and ask him to reveal himself to you through the word?

TESTIMONY OF APPLYING GOD'S WORD

As I meditated on Galatians 2:20 and it became planted on the inside of me, my focus became less on me and more on Jesus Christ. If Christ is in me (and he is), and he never changes (Hebrews 13:8), I knew I had a responsibility to learn more about him and what he did when he was on the earth. The more I learned, the more that I realized life wasn't just about me and my life. Isn't that a revelation? Yes, I was one of those who thought that my life and my circumstances was all that there was going on. Not totally, but you get the point.

In addition to God's word, listening to others who were advancing the kingdom, and reading countless books about men and women who let Christ manifest through their mortal bodies (2 Corinthians 4:10-11), I had an overwhelming sense of obligation and desire to do the same for my Lord.

One day I had stopped to get gas at a station where the attendant booth is between the sets of gas pumps. On the other side of the booth, I saw an older lady walking with a cane. I had just finished pumping my gas and was sitting in my truck. I knew what the Holy Spirit wanted to do. Do you know the scripture that says, *"...the spirit indeed is willing, but the flesh is weak"* (Matthew 26:41)? I sat there and argued with him in my mind.

As I looked to my right, there was a man sitting in his vehicle giving me an evil eye. I knew it was the enemy trying to stop me from doing what the Holy Spirit wanted to do through me. The Holy Spirit reminded me of Galatians 2:20. It wasn't about me, but that it was Christ in me. It was what he was desiring to do through me. He needed my participation since I was the temple, the vessel that he wanted to work through in that moment. Do you see how that changes things? It did for me, anyway.

I told the Holy Spirit that if there was a parking place next to the pump where the woman with the cane was, I would get out and pray for her. Well, guess what? As I pulled around, the vehicle that was next to hers pulled forward. I parked, got out, and timidly walked around to the gas pump where she was standing. Walking up to strangers was intimidating to me in the beginning of doing this. I said to her, "Excuse me. May I ask why you're walking with a cane?" She smiled telling me she had been in a car accident four months before and was still suffering with pain. I shared with her the word about God's will for her healing and asked if I could pray for her. I also asked for her first name. She readily said yes to the prayer, and do you know what her name was? Grace. Isn't that just like our Father? I prayed like Jesus taught us in Mark 11:22-24. She told me that she believed the things that I shared, we hugged, and then parted ways.

A week later, I was in the store where I had gotten gas. Guess who I saw walking down the aisle? Yes! There was Grace. I asked how she was doing and she said, "Look, no cane." She told me that all the pain was gone. She thanked me again for praying for her. I had never seen this woman before the day I was getting gas, and a week later God gives me the divine encounter with her to see his word at work. Isn't that awesome? I've never seen her again since.

Early in my experience hearing from the Lord, a battle, or really a bargaining session, would take place in my mind with God because I didn't want to step out and pray for a total stranger. However, the Holy Spirit would bring back the word (Galatians 2:20) to my remembrance, and from that encounter with the word (Jesus), I would be obedient.

APPLICATION ASSIGNMENT

1. Get in your quiet place with your Bible, journal, and pen.

2. Read John 14:26 and ask the Holy Spirit to reveal himself to you as Comforter.

3. Humble yourself and invite him to be your teacher.

4. Tell him that you trust in the word that he will bring scriptures back to your memory as you sow them in your heart. From now on, you will not say that you can't remember scriptures.

5. Ask your Father what scripture he wants you to sow in your heart today.

6. Write down what he gives to you.

CHAPTER 6

YOUR PART: I AM BORN AGAIN, NOW WHAT?

So, you have read in some of the scriptures about what happened when you said yes to Jesus. You then were given scriptures to describe the Holy Spirit who moved in to your temple, as well as some of the benefits of his relationship with you. What do you do with all of this information? Hopefully, you are doing the application assignments, which will help you not to be a hearer only, but a doer of the word (James 1:22). These assignments encourage the relationship and dependency on the Holy Spirit as you seek to develop the communication through the word.

Solomon tells us in Proverbs 23:7 that as a man thinks in his heart, so is he. The majority of us have had, or still have wrong thinking as it pertains to God's word. Areas of our lives that do not line up with the finished work of the cross can be attributed to destructive thoughts. Another way to look at it is through what Hosea 4:6 says, *"My people are destroyed for lack of knowledge: because thou hast rejected knowledge..."*

How do we change our way of thinking? How do we obtain the kind of knowledge that will produce the promises that are all yes and amen (2 Corinthians 1:20)?

This knowledge comes by way of presenting your body a living sacrifice, and by renewing your mind.

> *I beseech you therefore, brethren, by the mercies of*
> *God, that ye present your bodies a living sacrifice, holy,*
> *acceptable unto God, which is your reasonable service.*
> *And be not conformed to this world: but be ye transformed*
> *by the renewing of your mind, that ye may prove what*
> *is that good, and acceptable, and perfect, will of God.*
> (Romans 12:1-2)

First, you have to take time out of your busy schedule, get your Bible, open it up, and read it. For a lot of us, it starts out as a sacrifice because our flesh does not want to take the time to read what God has to say. We then begin to make excuses of why we don't have the time, and just settle in to hearing the preacher's message on Sunday morning, and we feel that we have accomplished our goal as a Christian. I was once that person. Since I was not raised in church, I really thought that I had become the epitome of a Christian when I started attending Sunday services on a regular basis. Isn't that arrogant? It's foolish also!

What do you think about the part in Romans 12:1 that says to present your body a living sacrifice? A lot of people are confused by this. The body being "sacrificed" here is our flesh, our physical part that needs to step out and physically walk, talk, communicate, and "be" with another person to love, forgive, and be humble and merciful sometimes against our will. Since our body is the temple, it's up to us to physically move it around on the earth to accomplish God's will through the Holy Spirit living inside of us.

Most of us are of the mindset that stepping out to be of service to another person in God's grace and humility is "going above and beyond" type of behavior, which borders on a works mentality. But Jesus is saying this is the least that's expected of born-again believers, i.e. our "reasonable service." This is the role we were born to play.

The second part of this process is not being conformed to the ways of the world, not thinking like the world thinks, or being in the pattern of this world. This is accomplished through the renewing of your mind. When you renew your mind, you are able to prove God's perfect will. How many times have we indicated that we don't know God's will about something? He just told us how to prove his will, and there are no exceptions or exclusions listed in this scripture.

The question then should be asked, "What is renewing our mind, and how do we do it?" So many times we read something and skim right over it, not asking the questions that will give us the practical and spiritual application, with understanding, that can only come by way of help from the Holy Spirit. I want to remind you to ask him to guide you into truth as you read the scriptures.

In my relationship with him, he will generally ask me a question as a means of getting me to engage him for understanding and clarification regarding a scripture. Isn't that how Jesus taught?

Let's look at the practical, kingdom principle that Jesus taught on how to renew our mind, and to produce the fruit of his promises in our lives. Before we look at this parable, do you know that if you are born again, you have already been *"delivered from the power of darkness, and translated into the kingdom of his dear Son"* (Colossians 1:13). You are already in the kingdom of Jesus Christ. You are not waiting to enter into this kingdom when you die and go to heaven. You are already in this kingdom.

Have you ever been to another country? Do you find it necessary to know how you should conduct yourself based on the laws of that country? How about the currency? What about the language? These are some of the areas that you might research before traveling to a country with different laws.

Now that you are aware, based on scripture, that you are in another kingdom (king's domain), aren't you just a tiny bit curious as to how this kingdom functions? You are now a fellow citizen with the saints (Ephesians 2:19, Philippians 3:20). Jesus tells us in Mark 4:11, *"Unto you it is given to know the mystery of the kingdom of God..."* He says it is for us to know how the kingdom operates. He also indicates that if you don't understand the parable that he is about to explain, you won't understand the others that he teaches (verse 13).

Mark 4 is one of my favorite parables that I constantly read, share, and teach. This is how to change the way you think (renewing your mind) that will line up with how the government of God's kingdom works:

The sower soweth the word. (Mark 4:14)

You are the sower responsible for sowing the word in your heart. In the next verses he explains the various soil (meaning your heart) conditions. All four heard the same word, but only the fourth soil produced the harvest. Jesus said, *"And these are they which are sown on good ground; such as hear the word, and receive it,* (Matthew 13:23 says *"understands it"*) *and bring forth fruit..."* (Mark 4:20). It is written in 2 Peter 1:3-4 that *"he has given unto us all things that pertain unto life and godliness, through the knowledge of him...whereby are given unto us exceeding great and precious promises..."*

How then are we to participate in these promises? First, you have to read about your inheritance to know about the promises, which can only be found in the Bible. Second, when you locate a promise (seed) that you are looking for, it must go from your eyes into your heart. Read how Solomon explained this process:

> *My son, attend to my **words**; incline thine ear unto my sayings. Let them not depart from thine eyes; keep them in the **midst of thine heart**. For they are **life** unto those that find them, and **health to all their flesh**. Keep thy **heart** with all diligence; for out of it are the issues of* life.
> (Proverbs 4:20-23 emphasis added)

Do you see the process in Solomon's words? It's the **word in your heart** that produces the promise, the life, the health, or whatever is needed. Do you see the importance of guarding your heart which determines the condition of it? Jesus explained this same process in Mark 4.

Let's look at another example of this process of renewing your mind in Joshua 1:8:

> *This book of the law shall not depart out of thy mouth; but thou shalt **meditate** therein **day and night**, that thou mayest observe to **do** according to all that is written therein: for **then** thou shalt make thy way **prosperous**, and then thou shalt have **good success**.* (emphasis added)

God is showing us many times through various places how to renew our minds and participate in the promises of his kingdom. It comes through his word in our hearts. If you still aren't convinced, I'll give you one more example found in Psalms 1:1-3:

> *Blessed is the man that walketh not in the counsel of the ungodly, nor standeth in the way of sinners, nor sitteth in the seat of the scornful. But his delight is in the **law of the Lord**; and in his law doth he **meditate day and night**. And he shall be like a tree planted by the rivers of water, that bringeth forth his fruit in his season; his leaf also shall not wither; and **whatsoever he doeth shall prosper***. (emphasis added)

When you meditate on God's word, you will prosper in every area of your life. This is how God's kingdom operates. You are a citizen of this kingdom. This is one of the ways that his kingdom comes, and his will is done on the earth as it is in heaven (Matthew 6:10). His children reveal his will when they get the word in them and produce the fruit of his promises. Look what Jesus said in Matthew 24:14:

> *And this **gospel of the kingdom** shall be preached in all the world for a witness unto all nations; and then shall the end come*. (emphasis added)

We can't ignore the truth that Jesus is the word (John 1:1, John 1:14). In God's sovereignty, he set his kingdom up in this way. May we humble ourselves and continue to sow the word in our hearts so that we can produce the fruit of his promises. When others see the hope that is in us and ask us about it, with meekness we can tell them (1 Peter 3:15) who our king is, and how his kingdom can work in their lives.

TESTIMONY OF APPLYING GOD'S WORD

As I began to sow the word in my heart, I realized how many wrong thoughts were inside of me, and how worldly they all were. Based on this type of thinking, I was making poor and ungodly choices. (And to think that I was actually a Christian!) The following two scriptures became very real in my thought life, and explain how the Holy Spirit began to teach me in my everyday decisions:

> *For the word of God is quick, and powerful, and sharper than any twoedged sword, piercing even to the dividing asunder of soul and spirit, and of the joints and marrow, and is a **discerner** of the **thoughts** and **intents of the heart**.* (Hebrews 4:12 emphasis added)

> *All scripture is given by inspiration of God, and is profitable for doctrine, for reproof, for correction, for **instruction in righteousness**: that the man of God may be perfect, thoroughly furnished unto all good works.* (2 Timothy 3:16 emphasis added)

When my son was younger, the pirate theme was very popular. Cartoons, commercials, costumes, coloring books, toys, and songs were inundated with images of the marauding character. With that kind of marketing, what do you think my son wanted as the theme for his birthday party? Pirates, of course, with a treasure chest design on the homemade cake, and all the related theme accessories that accompany this type of celebration. He then decided he wanted to have his room decorated in a pirate motif. As I began to search for room ideas, the Holy Spirit lead me to a scripture by way of a preacher on television who read the scripture in Isaiah 5:20:

> *Woe unto them that call evil good, and good evil...*

Can I admit to you that when I heard that scripture it pierced my soul! I knew what the Holy Spirit was trying to teach me in that one scripture. He then instructed me to look in the dictionary for the meaning of a pirate. I'll list it for you so you can see what I saw in that memorable teaching moment: *A robber on the high seas; one that by open violence takes the property of another on the high seas. In strictness, the word pirate is one who makes it his business to cruise for robbery or plunder; a freeboater on the seas. (Webster's Dictionary 1828 - Online Edition,* s.v. "pirate," accessed August 20, 2018, http://webstersdictionary1828.com/Dictionary/pirate)

Are you kidding me? How did I get suckered into believing the lie that pirates were cute and harmless? It's no different than the television shows that are calling witches, good; or the movies that portray vampires to be funny; or that witchcraft is cool for teenagers. Evil and deception are after our children's minds. Needless to say, the pirate theme came to a screeching halt in our home. I spent several weeks teaching my son what God's word said about what we watch, and how to discern good and evil.

Do you see how the word will work in your life under the guidance and direction of the Holy Spirit? He will show you where your thinking is wrong and how it is hindering your ability to grow in spiritual principles of the kingdom. I get corrected on a regular basis, or should I say, a daily basis.

APPLICATION ASSIGNMENT

1. Get in your quiet place with your Bible, journal, and pen.

2. Ask the Holy Spirit to reveal to you one area where your thinking is contrary to his word.

3. Ask him for a scripture that shows you what God says, his truth, about this area of wrong thinking.

4. Write down what he says to you. Meditate on the scripture and sow it in your heart. Begin to speak that particular promise/scripture out of your mouth. Remember, faith comes by hearing, and hearing the word of God (Romans 10:17). When we speak it out of our mouth, we hear that word being spoken. This is the process that was discussed in Mark 4:11-20, Joshua 1:8, Proverbs 4:20-23, and Psalms 1:1-3.

5. Enjoy the process of seed, time, and harvest (Genesis 8:22).

CHAPTER 7

YOUR PART: DESIRING THE SINCERE MILK OF THE WORD

As I began to understand how the word of God was used to change my wrong thought patterns, I couldn't get enough of the word. I then went through a frustration period where I didn't feel that the process was going fast enough. The Holy Spirit began to enlighten my understanding through gardening. God spoke this process in Genesis 8:22:

> *While the earth remaineth, seedtime and harvest, and*
> *cold and heat, and summer and winter, and day and*
> *night shall not cease.*

Do you see it? It is seed, time, and harvest. We have become such an instant gratification society. Who wants the "time" part? Let God's word be true and every man a liar (Romans 3:4). Jesus explained the time element further in Mark 4:28:

> *For the earth bringeth forth fruit of herself; first the blade,*
> *then the ear, after that the full corn in the ear.*

I have planted corn and I can tell you that it does not grow overnight. It is a process of getting the seed, preparing the soil, planting the seed, watering the ground, weeding around the plant as it grows (the worst part), and then one day you start to see the ear producing. But it's still not ready to eat. The ear has to fully grow without being taken by racoons. Do you know that the harvest time can be the busiest? The whole crop of corn grows to maturity at once, and then you have to do something with it. I am not a commercial farmer, so the corn I grow is for personal consumption. I now have to harvest the whole crop of corn.

Jesus used natural illustrations that one could see and understand to explain the spiritual principles of his kingdom. It is the role of the Holy Spirit to guide you into these truths so that you can apply them in your own life. However, God has given you the choice to sow to the world's way of doing things, or sow to his kingdom way of living life. His love for you does not change, but boy does your life change when you cooperate with the principles found in his word!

Did you notice the title of this chapter? Following along in the reality that this is a process of reaping the harvest of God's promises that are sown in your heart, look at some confirming scriptures:

> As newborn babes, **desire the sincere milk of the word**, that ye may **grow** thereby: If so be ye have tasted that the Lord is gracious. (1 Peter 2:2-3 emphasis added)

> I have fed you with **milk**, and not with meat: for hitherto ye were not able to bear it, neither yet now are ye able. For ye are yet carnal: for whereas there is among you envying, and strife, and divisions, are ye not carnal, and walk as men? (1 Corinthians 3:2-3 emphasis added)

> For when for the time ye ought to be teachers, ye have need that one teach you again which be the first principles of the oracles of God; and are become such as have **need of milk**, and not of strong meat. For every one that **useth milk is unskillful in the word of righteousness**: for he is a babe. But strong meat belongeth to them that are of full age, even those who by reason of use have their senses exercised to discern both good and evil. (Hebrews 5:12-14 emphasis added)

*Whom shall he teach knowledge? And whom shall he make to understand doctrine? Them that are weaned from the **milk**, and drawn from the breasts. For precept must be upon precept; line upon line, line upon line; here a little, and there a little...* (Isaiah 28:9-10 emphasis added)

Can you see the necessary steps for growth? It is the same in the natural with a newborn baby. You can't shove solid food in a baby's mouth. You nourish the baby along with milk.

As I began the journey in the word, I was trying to sow many seeds at once in the garden of my heart. One night, I had a dream that I was shoving huge amounts of ground meat into the microwave. The meat was oozing out the sides and door. I opened the door and some of the meat was cooked, and the rest was still raw. The Holy Spirit gently spoke to me that I was trying to process too much at one time. He has constantly reminded me that this is a journey that involves time. I want to take this moment to encourage you with this truth as well. You can't compare yourself as you see others harvesting and enjoying the fruit of the promises.

*For we dare not make ourselves of the number, or compare ourselves with some that commend themselves: but they measuring themselves by themselves, **and comparing themselves among themselves, are not wise.***
(2 Corinthians 10:12 emphasis added)

They went through the seed, time, and harvest action plan just like you are doing now. This planting process is for every type of harvest that you want in God's plethora of promises. Many have said that they tried memorizing the scriptures and confessing with their mouth, but it didn't work. I like what my husband's response is in these conversations. "You just called God a liar." If you really want to understand this kingdom principle of sowing, plant a garden with the Holy Spirit as your master gardener. He will walk you through with his wisdom and revelation in the natural and the kingdom to yield a harvest in both!

Remember what the writer of Hebrews said that one who is on milk is "unskilled in the word of righteousness?" What is righteousness? A simple definition for me is doing what is right according to what God's word says. Before I started feeding on the word of God, I would have recurring dreams that as I was talking, my teeth were falling out. I would catch one or two in my hand and attempt to put them back in my mouth as I continued in the conversation. I hated those dreams! Guess what? I quit having them as I began to renew my mind to the word and apply it in my life. Look at how this maturing process works in 2 Peter 1:2-8:

> *Grace and peace* **be multiplied** *unto you through the* **knowledge** *of God, and of Jesus our Lord, according as his divine power hath given unto us* **all things that pertain unto life and godliness, through the knowledge of** **him** *that hath called us to glory and virtue: whereby are given unto us* **exceeding great and precious promises***: that by these ye might be partakers of the divine nature, having escaped the corruption that is in the world through lust. And beside this, giving all diligence,* **add to your faith** *virtue; and to virtue knowledge; and to knowledge temperance; and to temperance patience; and to patience godliness; and to godliness brotherly kindness; and to brotherly kindness charity. For if these things be in you, and abound, they make you that ye shall neither be barren nor unfruitful in the knowledge of our Lord Jesus Christ. (emphasis added)*

There are so many amazing truths and nuggets in these scriptures. I just want to make a few points. Many people asking for prayer desire peace in their life. First of all, peace is a fruit of the Holy Spirit (Galatians 5:22). The Prince of Peace resides in the born-again believer (Galatians 2:20, Isaiah 9:6-7). Jesus said that he has given us his peace (John 14:27).

Second, look how Peter says that grace and peace is multiplied to you. What is zero times zero? Zero. Peace is already in your born-again spirit by way of the Holy Spirit. That's why Peter can say that there will be a multiplication factor as you obtain knowledge about God and Jesus our Lord. How do you obtain that knowledge into your soul? By getting into his word, sowing it into your heart, meditating on it, believing it, confessing it with your mouth, and guarding your heart.

Why did Peter say, "...add to your faith?" What is one of the fruits of the Holy Spirit? Faith (Galatians 5:22). Whose faith do you now live by? By the faith of the Son of God (Galatians 2:20). This list that Peter gives to us is instruction in righteousness (2 Timothy 3:16), and teaching us the process of becoming skilled in the word of righteousness. This is character development in the making; growing us up in our soul into the image of Christ. It all has to do with knowledge that comes from God's word.

TESTIMONY OF APPLYING GOD'S WORD

I love hearing other people's testimonies of how they pursued the Lord through his word, and the results of those pursuits. We even find ourselves laughing at their "growing pains." Right? I enjoy talking about most of the experiences I've had with the Holy Spirit, however some are not very pleasant to share. You will have those also as you journey in this kingdom endeavor of maturity.

When Harold and I married, I knew Psalms 23 and John 3:16. Harold, on the other hand, had been teaching Sunday school, Bible studies, preaching messages, and walking in wisdom for many years. Do you get the picture? He was attending a nondenominational church and was best friends with the pastor. When the pastor left town, Harold would preach. He led a Bible study on Tuesday evening. He spent many years ministering God's word in people's everyday lives and struggles.

There was a lady in our community who moved from another state when she married a local man she met on the internet. She had been part of the Mormon church, dabbled in the occult, and regularly spewed her hatred for the Jews. She and her new husband started coming to church when he was charged with stealing heavy equipment and taking it across state lines. They also attended Harold's Bible study. She was a tall overbearing woman who was full of rage. She intimidated me on many levels. I would cringe every time she opened her mouth.

One day she called my house when Harold was at work. She wanted to know if I would answer a few questions regarding the Bible. In my prideful, all-knowing self I said yes. I was hopeful that she truly was seeking God's way of doing things. Before she arrived, I explained to my son that she was coming and to stay in his room and play.

Let me take a short detour in the testimony. My son asked me one day if the devil made his dad cuss. I took a brief moment and asked the Holy Spirit for help in providing an answer to my son who was three at the time. I told him that the devil doesn't make him do anything. I gave him the illustration of his dad having a gate. The enemy could give him the idea to cuss, but that it was up to him to shut the gate to that idea and not cuss. We have gates in our pastures, so he understood the concept.

Now, back to the testimony. The lady's voice began to raise as she shared her hatred of people in her past, the faults of her new husband, and a litany of other things that bothered her. I had my Bible open and tried several times to interrupt by redirecting her attention to what God said about her situations. But clearly she had not come to my house to hear about what God had to say.

My mind and body began to grow weary. At one point, I shut down internally. I had heard enough. I also did not want my son listening to the vitriol coming from this woman's mouth. I made some excuse that I needed to wrap things up, and she left. My son walked out of his room saying, "Mama, her gate was broken!" Is that discernment or what?

A few weeks later, the lady called asking if she could come over to talk to Harold. My head began to throb as resentment started to build. I did not want her in our house again. However, Harold and I agreed that she could come over, but that we visit outside on the porch, instead of allowing her energy inside our home.

When she arrived, she immediately began to dictate to Harold what she wanted him to teach on Tuesday night at Bible study because she felt it would properly instruct her husband whom she believed was stealing from her. I was appalled. I was witnessing manipulation rising up in her against my husband. She began to spew again while Harold attentively listened. I, on the other hand, did not want to be an audience to this outburst. I knew only a few scriptures, so my "instruction in righteousness," i.e. scriptures sown in my heart, was not fully developed or mature enough for me to discern how to act in this situation. So you know what I did? I got angry and began to explain to her in not so many ways "how the cow ate the cabbage." That's southern for "giving her a piece of my mind."

The woman stood up abruptly, her anger intensifying. But, she stopped spewing because, well, mine took over. When I finished, she turned on her heel and stormed off. Harold followed her to her vehicle. As she opened the car door and proceeded to get in she told him through clenched teeth that I was to never speak to her again.

Harold was clearly upset with me and told me that our witness with her was ruined. (Neither of us were convinced that she was saved.) He then left to go take our garbage to the dump, and I got on the riding lawn mower with my head still throbbing. I cried out to the Lord asking him why this happened. He gently told me that what I was discerning was correct. But my speech and choice of deliverance, was not.

That night I had a dream. In the sky was written, "Numbers." The next morning, the Holy Spirit spoke to me through the preacher on television, using James 1:19-20:

> Wherefore, my beloved brethren, let every man be swift to hear, slow to speak, slow to wrath: for the wrath of man worketh not the righteousness of God.

I failed that one! I then asked the Holy Spirit what my dream meant. He told me to read the book of Numbers in the Bible. Have you ever sat down to just read the book of Numbers? Neither had I. Guess how many chapters I had to get through before the piercing of the soul began? Nineteen! Here's where the sword hit its mark:

> And the Lord spake unto Moses, saying, Take the rod, and gather thou the assembly together, thou, and Aaron thy brother, **and speak, ye unto the rock** before their eyes; and it shall give forth his water... (Numbers 20:7-8 emphasis added)

> And Moses and Aaron gathered the congregation together before the rock, and he said unto them, Hear now, ye rebels; must we fetch you water out of this rock? And

*Moses lifted up his hand, and with his rod he **smote the
rock twice**...* (Numbers 20:10-11 emphasis added)

God instructed Moses to speak to the rock. Moses was angry with the people and hit the rock in anger, disobeying God. (You should go back and read the story.) He portrayed God to the children of Israel in a way that was not pleasing to God. Do you know what happened as a result of Moses' anger? He did not get to take the children of Israel into the promised land (Numbers 20:12). That was a severe consequence for Moses. Aren't you thankful for the blood of Jesus? I am.

As I read those scriptures, the Holy Spirit told me that I needed to call that woman and apologize to her for my anger. I began to cry. In my mind, I was trying to justify my anger and what I had said. But I knew that I needed to be obedient. War was raging in my members! My heart wanted to be obedient, but my flesh screamed, "No!" The Holy Spirit won out, however I prayed that she wouldn't answer the phone. I told the Lord that I was sorry for what I did. He reminded me that although he had forgiven me, she might not. I called and left a message apologizing for my anger. I never saw her again. We found out later that she and her husband moved out of state.

As I share this testimony with you, I am so thankful for where God has brought me from, where I am today, and where he's leading me to.

APPLICATION ASSIGNMENT

1. Ask the Holy Spirit to reveal to you one area in your life that you need to be instructed in righteousness.

2. Ask him to give you a scripture to support the corresponding directive in this area based on God's word of righteousness.

3. Write what he reveals to you in your journal.

4. Meditate on the scripture, sow it in your heart and let it change your thought patterns and behavior.

CHAPTER 8

YOUR PART: FREELY YOU HAVE RECEIVED, FREELY GIVE

After having a child of my own and watching other children, I can say that there is progression and a growth process. Sure, I am stating the obvious but making a comparison in spiritual growth. In most cases, children are eating solid food, walking, and making babbling sounds as they try to form a word or two by the time they are twelve to fifteen months old. By age three, a lot of growing in all areas has taken place. Would you agree? I am going by observation and experience, not scientific data.

How long was Jesus with his disciples teaching them how his unseen kingdom operated in the earthly realm? The consensus is around three-and-a-half years. His entire ministry was about other people. It focused on teaching, healing, and setting people free from the power of darkness. He was revealing the Father's love through giving. It is his nature. He is love (1 John 4:16). He loved and he gave (John 3:16). Jesus demonstrated this love in his ministry on the earth. It is now who we are in our born-again spirit.

Let's summarize a few things that God has freely given to us through the beating, death, and resurrection of his Son, Jesus Christ:

- His Son's life for the world because he loved us.
  (John 3:16, Galatians 2:20)
- We have redemption and the forgiveness of our sins.
  (Colossians 1:14)
- We have been reconciled to God by Jesus Christ.
  (2 Corinthians 5:18)
- He has given us the Holy Spirit of promise (Ephesians 1:13), the same Spirit that raised Christ from the dead. (Ephesians 1:18-20)
- He has delivered us from the power of darkness and placed us in his kingdom. (Colossians 1:13)
- He has given us his armor. (Ephesians 6:11)
- He said that all of his promises are yes and amen.
  (2 Corinthians 1:20)
- He has seated us in heavenly places and blessed us with all spiritual blessings. (Ephesians 1:3, 2:6)
- He told us to seek his kingdom first and his right way of doing things, and all things would be added to us. (Matthew 6:33, 1 Corinthians 3:21, 1 Timothy 6:17, 2 Peter 1:3-4, Philippians 4:19)
- He has given us many titles in his kingdom: king and priest (Revelation 1:6, 1 Peter 2:9); ambassador for Christ (2 Corinthians 5:20); a good soldier of Jesus Christ (2 Timothy 2:3); sons of God (Romans 8:14, Galatians 4:6, 1 John 3:2), and many others.

What are you lacking based on just these few scriptures? Nothing. Now, you may not be experiencing the promises in your life at the moment, but it's not because God is holding out and hasn't released them to you. They are truth according to God's word, but the process of receiving this truth—his promises—goes back to the process of sowing the word in your heart. Are you beginning to see clearly your role in God's sovereign plan? You do have a part to play in this relationship.

This is one of my favorite scriptures and is quoted from one of my favorite movies, *One Night with the King:*

It is the glory of God to conceal a thing: but the honour of
kings is to search out a matter. (Proverbs 25:2)

Have you freely received all of these things of him—from our Father—to just go to church (if you go to church), hear a message on Sunday, and live your life without a real purpose, plan, or destiny? What did Jesus say while he was teaching his disciples about the kingdom?

And as ye go, preach, saying, The kingdom of heaven
is at hand. Heal the sick, cleanse the lepers, raise the
dead, cast out devils: freely ye have received, freely give.
(Matthew 10:7-8)

Jesus was describing what the effects of his government looked like when it invaded the kingdom of darkness. If Jesus Christ is the same yesterday, today, and forever (Hebrews 13:8), and he is in us (Galatians 2:20), and his word never changes (Psalms 89:34, John 1:1, Isaiah 55:11), how can we quench the Holy Spirit in our lives (1 Thessalonians 5:19) when others are still bound by the power of darkness just like they were in the days that Jesus was on the earth?

Only the Holy Spirit can guide you into truth. However, Hosea 4:6 was very clear that the knowledge can still be rejected. You have in you the Spirit of the living God for a reason. It is not just so you can go be with the Lord when you die (2 Corinthians 5:8). That is a truth if you are born again.

As I began to see in the scriptures the love that God had for me, and all that he had provided for me to live in this life through Christ, I wanted to humble myself and be a willing vessel. I lived in the wilderness, walking in ignorance and arrogance for thirty-nine years. Yes, I was saved and Jesus was my Savior, but I did not allow him to be the Lord of my life. There is a difference.

The more I learned and continue to learn, the more I realize I don't know. The more I experience of him, the more dependent I become on him. The word began to change me on the inside. I became rooted and grounded in the love of Christ that passes "head knowledge" (Ephesians 3:17-19). I am still growing in this area and will for the rest of my life. However, as I received from him, it began to overflow and I had to share with others. I had to testify of his goodness. So many have a wrong perception of our Father because of experiences, wrong teaching, and/or ignorance to his word. I don't say this to be condemning. It's a fact that I have observed through the years in ministry.

TESTIMONIES OF APPLYING GOD'S WORD

Holy Spirit, I ask that you guide the reader into truth. Enlighten the eyes of understanding to see the power that is inside of him or her, and the power that is in God's word because Jesus is the word. In his name, I pray.

As I meditated on James 1:22, *"But be ye doers of the word, and not hearers only, deceiving your own selves,"* I realized that I had to start walking out what I was reading. I needed to start applying the word in everyday life. One of the areas where Harold and I focused early on in our spiritual walk together was healing. His first wife died as a result of the side effects of radiation as it tried to kill the cancer in her body. My desire was to learn how my son's healing was manifested in his body.

Many seek God's word when they have a need. Once the need has been met, some go on living their life as before. Others make it a daily walk and continue the pursuit of drawing closer to the One who so loves us. I chose the latter. Nonetheless, God's love is constant regardless of the path we choose.

As I learned about healing through scriptures such as Isaiah 53:3-5, Psalms 103:1-6, Psalms 107:20, Matthew 8:16-17, 1 Peter 2:24, and 3 John 2, just to name a few, I was fully persuaded (Romans 4:20-21) that God's word was true in the area of healing. Plus, I had a testimony of how it worked based on Mark 11:22-24 in my own life with my son's healed heart. Some of what I have learned I experienced first. Then I went to line up the experience with scripture.

One morning, Harold and I were driving our car on a busy street in Shreveport. All of a sudden, the man in the vehicle in front of us slammed on his brakes just as a pit bull ran in front of his car. As the man continued braking, the dog was in front of the tires being pushed by the vehicle as it was coming to a stop. Then the tire rolled over the dog. The dog got up and hobbled onto the sidewalk with his back leg flailing uncontrollably. The man pulled over onto the side street.

Knowing what I had learned about Christ in me, I told Harold that we had to stop and pray for the dog. He pulled onto the side street behind the man who ran over the dog. The driver, a big burly man with a ponytail, had gotten out of his car and was crying over what had just happened. Running down the street were some kids carrying a leash and screaming. They were the owners of the dog. The mom was running behind the kids, yelling at them over what just happened to her family's dog. Harold and I squatted down beside the injured animal. He had a lot of puncture wounds but not a single drop of blood oozed from his body. I was so thankful for that. Harold was positioned by the dog's head, and I was at his back end. By then, all of the members of the involved party were standing around us, including another man who appeared to be the father of the children.

Harold began to pray for the dog. As my eyes were closed, I saw that the dog had a lacerated liver. (Now, in the natural, I don't know what a liver looks like, much less one that is "lacerated"! However, in the Spirit you know all things. 1 John 2:20.) I began to speak healing on the liver using the principle that I had learned in Mark 11:22-24. A few minutes went by and Harold told me that it was time to let the dog get up. When he said that, the dog got up! No dangling back leg! He walked around perfectly fine. All I could say to the mama was, "It was Jesus!"

Harold and I got into the car speechless. He asked me, "Did you see the dog stretch out his hind leg?" I had my eyes closed so I missed that incredible detail! It was after that the Holy Spirit told Harold to let the dog get up. Yes, Jesus cares about the animals, but they have their proper place in God's sovereignty. God warned us of making our animals and pets more important than him. Romans 1:25 says some people worship the creature more than the Creator. God gave us the animals to enjoy in their proper place, and in this instance our prayer on the dog was effective. God used the whole incident as a witness of his love to the family of the dog and the man who ran over the dog.

This was our first public healing experience. Everyone needs their own testimonies. The only way that you will get them is to believe what God says about you and him. People can argue with your doctrines, your beliefs, but very few will argue with you regarding your testimony. They may not believe you, but they won't typically argue with you.

One afternoon, my son and I were on our way home from town and while sitting at a red light, I noticed the lady next to me in her car. She was pressing on her chest with a fearful expression on her face. The hospital was at the next red light. I told my son I was going to follow her and that if she pulled into the hospital parking lot, I would get out and pray for her. (He is quite accustomed to these spontaneous acts of faith and obedience.)

Sure enough, she turned into the hospital lot and parked. I was not able to find an open parking spot close to her, so I pulled into the handicap space up front and told my son that I would be right back. I walked slowly to give the woman time to get out of her vehicle so I wouldn't startle her and add to her already frightened state. As I came around the back of her car towards the driver's side door, I said, "Excuse me, do you need prayer?" She quickly responded in shock with what sounded like contempt, "Why would you ask me that?" Responding diffidently, I explained that I observed her at the red light pressing on her chest. She began to cry uncontrollably and share that a stent was placed in her heart a few months earlier. She had recently undergone a routine follow-up visit, and now her doctor was telling her that she needed to come in immediately.

I began to share with her about Jesus and the truth that he had paid for her right to walk in health. She asked me why I would follow a total stranger to pray for them in a parking lot. I told her it was because I was a Christian. She reassured me that she was a Christian as well but that she would never do what I was doing. I asked her if I could pray for her and she readily accepted.

By now, she had stopped crying enough so I could understand her when I asked for her first name. I prayed like Jesus taught us and commanded the spirit of fear to leave her (2 Timothy 1:7). I spoke God's word over her heart (Psalms 107:20). Her entire countenance had changed. I told her to walk into that hospital with her head high knowing that God sent a total stranger sitting at a red light to this divine appointment. She hugged me, we parted ways, and I've never seen her again.

I just love being a laborer with God through Jesus Christ (1 Corinthians 3:9). See, in his sovereignty, he chooses to operate through believers to accomplish his will on the earth as it is in heaven. Let me share one other testimony here.

Harold and I went to a conference in Dallas to listen to a ministry that believes that it is our responsibility to do the Great Commission that Jesus commanded in Mark 16:15-18. In the hotel lobby, I noticed a woman dressed in all white. She glowed. I remember thinking the words "purity and holiness." I was, and am still learning the voice and unction of the Holy Spirit.

The following day at the conference, a friend of ours asked if I would come and pray for a woman whom he had prayed for but hadn't received the results she needed. It was the lady I saw in the lobby. When I greeted her, she shared that she had not slept all night in more than forty years. How is that possible? She explained that she was tormented during the evening hours and could not sleep through an entire night. I asked her what happened forty years ago. She told me that she had been gang raped.

Oh no! How tragic! Do you see how crucial the timing of the Holy Spirit is in the moment? I wish I had spoken the words I heard about her the day before that might have encouraged her in the Lord. Remember the words purity and holiness that came into my born-again spirit? Look at what Proverbs 25:11 says, *"A word fitly spoken is like apples of gold in pictures of silver."*

I missed one opportunity to be lead by the Holy Spirit, but I was about to get another one. Harold and I learned that when a traumatic event occurs, there is a spirit of trauma that slips in and masks itself in various forms. I began to pray God's word over her and how he saw her in Christ. At the moment that I sensed the Holy Spirit's unction, I commanded that spirit of trauma to leave her. She began to shake and tremble and asked me what was going on. I had never experienced this before when praying with someone. When she calmed down, I hugged her and she began to cry. The Holy Spirit gave me words of edification to speak to her. It was a time of love and compassion for her to experience freedom from that event that had her bound all of those years. Perfect love casts out all fear (1 John 4:18).

The next morning, she walked up to me with tears in her eyes. She said that she slept all night for the first time in forty years. We hugged and she thanked me for the prayers. Oh, how good the indwelling Holy Spirit is to me! It is so humbling to realize that he is the one working through you when you present your body a living sacrifice (Romans 12:1). When I began to see Jesus first and to pursue him with all of my heart, my focus was no longer on me and my life. What an amazing journey it is!

APPLICATION ASSIGNMENT

1. Ask the Holy Spirit to give you an opportunity to speak edification to a total stranger. Remember, there is no more sure word of prophecy than the word of God (2 Peter 1:19). What is prophecy? Paul says that it is edification, exhortation, and comfort (1 Corinthians 14:3). God's word will build up, draw one in, and comfort the hearer. You can never go wrong by speaking scripture to someone. Remember, it is Christ in you. One has to get over the fear of man in order to be obedient to the Holy Spirit. *The fear of man bringeth a snare: but whoso putteth his trust in the Lord shall be safe"* (Proverbs 29:25).

2. Journal your journey. Over the years, I have written down the things that the Lord teaches me, including my dreams, visions, etc. Nearly every morning, I kneel beside my bed with my face down on the floor, with my journal by my side. I write down what my Father speaks to me for the day. You don't need someone else's daily devotional when you have direct access to the Father. I'm not against devotionals; it's just that it is so lovely to go to God yourself and receive directly from him. If you're not there yet, keep pursuing. You will get there as long as you continue to seek (Matthew 7:7). I have also encouraged my son to do this as well. One day he asked me why I had him do this. I responded that the way God speaks to him is how God would speak to others through him. Our Father is always loving, even when he is correcting us. We need to communicate to others like he does with us.

CHAPTER 9

YOUR PART: THE RIGHTEOUS ARE BOLD AS A LION

Have you ever pictured Jesus with a whip, driving people and animals out of the temple, and overthrowing tables? Read John 2:15-17. I would call that righteous indignation being displayed by Jesus. That was some boldness in action. What about when he was having the conversation with the Pharisees (the religious order of the day)? Look what Jesus says to the religious leaders in John 8:43-45, emphasis added:

> *Why do ye not understand my speech? Even because ye cannot hear my word.* **Ye are of your father the devil,** *and the lusts of your father ye will do. He was a murderer from the beginning, and abode not in the truth, because there is no truth in him. When he speaketh a lie, he speaketh of his own: for he is a liar, and the father of it.*
> *And because I tell you the truth, ye believe me not.*

Look at the boldness of Jesus in this example! Can you imagine someone saying this to religious leaders today who refuse to hear and believe the truth of God's word?

Solomon writes that the righteous are bold as a lion (Proverbs 28:1). Is the question, where are the righteous today? Or is the question, where are the ones who are righteous and bold? What happened to your yes being yes, and your no being no (James 5:12)?

We are instructed to abhor evil, and to cleave to that which is good (Romans 12:9). There is boldness needed to hate evil and to stand against it. Look what the Lord hates in Proverbs 6:16-19:

> *These six things doth the Lord hate: yea, seven are an abomination unto him: a proud look, a lying tongue, and hands that shed innocent blood, an heart that deviseth wicked imaginations, feet that be swift in running to mischief, a false witness that speaketh lies, and he that soweth discord among brethren.*

It takes boldness to stand against the things that our Lord hates. We also have to constantly be reminded that our struggle is not against flesh and blood (Ephesians 6:12). Our struggle is not people; our battle is spiritual. This is where you can make the mental switch in your imagination that you are a good soldier.

> *Thou therefore endure hardness, as a good soldier of Jesus Christ. No man that warreth entangleth himself with the affairs of this life; that he may please him who hath chosen him to be a soldier.* (2 Timothy 2:3-4)

How many things, activities, and battles are we involved with that we have no business being in? That is just a side question based on the following scripture. What things are we engaged in that are keeping our focus on temporal issues instead of eternal things?

> *While we look not at the things which are seen, but at the things which are not seen: for the things which are seen are temporal; but the things which are not seen are eternal.* (2 Corinthians 4:18)

So, where should our focus be as a good soldier of Jesus Christ? His word, and he is his word (John 1:1, John 1:14). His word is spirit (eternal) and life (John 6:63).

When Harold joined the army, he became the property of the United States military. He was told what to eat, when to eat, what to wear, where to go, etc. When you said yes to Jesus, you were translated into his kingdom, his government (Colossians 1:13). Look how Paul describes you:

> *Ye are bought with a price; be not ye the servants of men. Brethren, let every man, wherein he is called, therein abide with God.* (1 Corinthians 7:23-24)

> *What? Know ye not that your body is the temple of the Holy Ghost which is in you, which ye have of God, and ye are not your own? For ye are bought with a price: therefore glorify God in your body, and in your spirit, which are God's.* (1 Corinthians 6:19-20)

What are you doing with God's body? These scriptures are very clear that your body is not your own anymore. It was paid for through the shed blood of our Lord and Savior Jesus Christ, your Commander in Chief. What kind of damage are you doing to this body that houses his Spirit?

We have all been guilty of doing reckless, harmful, ungodly things with our body (his temple) even after we were born again. However, truth will set you free from the guilt and shame. Confess where you missed the mark and close the door to the enemy. Stand up, dust yourself off, put on God's armor (his word), and engage the enemy in order to set others free.

You are in a battle whether you want it or not, believe it or not, or rather you choose to ignore it. Why do you think Paul said to fight the good fight of faith in 1 Timothy 6:12? Why are we told to put on armor in Ephesians 6:11? By the way, did you notice that he told you to put it on? God's not going to do what he told you to do. See, you have a part to play in God's sovereignty. Look how Peter, in addition to what Paul says, informs us on who our enemy is:

> *Be sober, be vigilant; because your adversary the devil, as a roaring lion, walketh about, seeking whom he may devour: whom resist stedfast in the faith, knowing that the same afflictions are accomplished in your brethren that are in the world.* (1 Peter 5:8-9)

Did you notice that the devil is not after believers who conform to the world and look like the world? He is after those who are resisting him by believing God's word. We are told to submit to God, resist the devil and he will flee from us (James 4:7). Notice again, you have to resist the devil. Why do you think God gave you his Spirit, his word (the sword), and permission to use the name of Jesus Christ (John 16:23)? It is so that you can resist the devil and he will flee from you.

You have everything that you need to be more than a conqueror through him that loved you (Romans 8:37). This is why you can be thankful in all things (1 Thessalonians 5:18) because he causes us always to triumph in Christ (2 Corinthians 2:14). Do you see the military terms in the scriptures? My husband said that he was trained and equipped for battle. However, he indicated the greatest fear of the military is that the soldier would not engage the enemy. Is that not a picture of the Christian today?

Most are blaming God when the attacks come in their life. I am going to share what God says regarding the lies that the enemy has fed to the Christian. As long as you think it is God allowing, doing, and/or causing the attack to teach you something, you will not rise up as a soldier of Jesus Christ and resist the enemy. You have to rightly divide the word of truth (2 Timothy 2:15). We are after the cross, and in a better covenant that is established upon better promises (Hebrews 8:6).

> *The thief cometh not, but for to steal, and to kill, and to destroy: I am come that they might have life, and that they might have it more abundantly.* (John 10:10)

In my Bible, these words are written in red. That means Jesus said these words. He came to give life, not take it. He doesn't take our health, our children, our finances, or anything else. He is a giver! He gave his life for you. He gave us his word to teach us, not sickness or disease.

> *Let no man say when he is tempted, I am tempted of God: for God cannot be tempted with evil, **neither tempteth he any man**: But every man is tempted, when he is **drawn away of his own lust**, and enticed. Then when lust hath conceived, it bringeth forth sin: and sin,*

when it is finished, bringeth forth death. (James 1:13-15 emphasis added)

How clear are these scriptures? God doesn't tempt man with evil. Look at what God says next:

> *Do not err, my beloved brethren. Every good gift and every perfect gift is from above, and cometh down from the Father of lights, with whom is no variableness, neither shadow of turning.* (James 1:16-17)

Don't be mistaken, God isn't tempting you. Everything that he gives is good and comes from him. Remember, he is light and in him is no darkness at all (1 John 1:5). You have to understand that there are natural and spiritual laws that are applicable to everything in life. In this particular subject matter, there is sowing and reaping:

> *Be not deceived; God is not mocked: for whatsoever a man soweth, that shall he also reap. For he that soweth to his flesh shall of the flesh reap corruption; but he that soweth to the Spirit shall of the Spirit reap life everlasting.* (Galatians 6:7-8)

When we sow to our flesh, from our flesh we reap corruption. It is not from God! I pray that this is a revelation to you if you struggle in the area regarding God's role in evil.

God is love and God is light. His righteous justice will prevail. Read the book of Revelation to see how evil is dealt with once and for all. However, as a believer of Jesus Christ in the here and now, it is no longer you that lives, but Christ lives in you (Galatians 2:20). Jesus came to destroy the works of the devil (1 John 3:8), so there is still work to be done in setting the captives free. Soldier, submit yourself to God. Receive his love; stand up and engage the one who keeps stealing, killing, and destroying on your watch.

As you sow seeds (the word of God) in your heart regarding his love for you, your line of thinking starts to change. The Holy Spirit is able to reveal the deep things of God to you (1 Corinthians 2:10). When you are able to see your Father as good and that his love is unconditional, you can *"go boldly unto the throne of grace, obtain mercy and find grace to help in time of need"* (Hebrews 4:16). Because of Christ Jesus our Lord, *"we have boldness and access with confidence by the faith of him"* (Ephesians 3:12).

We will never walk in all that Jesus died and paid for as long as we have a wrong thought life regarding our Father. We also will not fulfill the destiny that he has specifically chosen for us as long as our focus is on us and our failures, past, sins, etc. Embrace truth and reject the lies. Sow the word of God in your heart. Humble yourself and cooperate with the principles of his kingdom. Be who God made you to be in Jesus Christ.

TESTIMONY OF APPLYING GOD'S WORD

I am going to share a testimony with you about the day the Lord wanted me to wear camouflage pants to church. This powerful experience took me to a deeper level of understanding on how spiritual things work, both good and bad. I felt the power and the anointing of the Holy Spirit like never before in my life.

Harold and I had been married a little more than a year. I was a new wife to this man of God who held a leadership position in his church. Harold's walk with Christ is one of the qualities that attracted me to him. Through his prompting and my pursuing I was growing by leaps and bounds in my knowledge of God's love for me.

I was also learning to hear the Holy Spirit as the words in the Bible were coming alive to me in my heart. I recall vividly one morning getting in my prayer position, which is down on my knees with my face on the floor, and proclaiming to the Lord that I would submit my whole life to him. I felt I needed to declare this because while I knew Jesus was my Savior, I had not yet made him Lord over all of my life. And I had not yet renewed my mind to everything he had already given to me. So, on that day I told God that whatever I needed, I would trust that he would give it to me. I arose from my prayer time with him and went about my day.

One Sunday later on, Harold and I got up to get ready for church. While taking a shower that morning, I began to see an image of myself standing on the platform in the sanctuary in front of the congregation praying out loud for certain people. It was a thought that took me completely off guard because I'm normally a quiet church-goer who minds her own business. Plus, up to this point in my spiritual walk, I had stepped out and prayed in person for someone just one time in my life, so you can imagine my surprise when such a thought popped in my head. Sensing it might be from the Holy Spirit, I declared out loud in defiance, "Not me!" But this image of me standing before the whole audience would not leave. In my mind, I told the Holy Spirit that I did not feel comfortable doing something like that.

Remember, I'm the wife of a man who is in leadership at this church. He likes to sit in the front row, so dutifully I join him by his side. I was still getting accustomed to my position as the spouse of a man of God who has influence in our congregation. All this was a new mindset for me because before I met Harold, I was a sometime church-goer who'd slip in the side door and find a seat in the back.

This country church had a regular attendance of about eighty people. In my time going there, I'd say hello to the door greeters, make some small talk, and then Harold and I would take our seats up front. Just to give you an idea of the culture of the church, I observed that on a regular basis a particular husband and wife, who were separated at the time, attended church each on their own. They sat on opposite sides of the sanctuary and would not speak to one other. They were adamant that during their separation they both wanted to continue attending church. To me, this seemed like a whole lot of drama for such a small church that no one appeared to address in the form of prayer.

One day as I was walking down the hallway, I felt the unction to pull the wife aside and pray for her and her marriage. (This is that one time I stepped out to pray for someone in person.) At that time, I was unsure of actually how to pray or what to say, but I knew I had to be obedient to the Holy Spirit who was nudging me to do this. By the expression on her face, she was shocked that I would ask to pray for her. Imagine that! In a church, someone is surprised when asked if they could be prayed for!

Now, back to the Sunday morning part of the testimony where I wore camouflage pants. After my shower, I walked to my closet. As I stood in front of it trying to decide what to wear, my eyes were directed to the stack of blue jeans folded neatly on the top shelf. In the midst of those jeans were a pair of camouflage pants that I had bought years ago to wear playing paintball. The Holy Spirit within me directed me to wear those pants. My heart rate accelerated. I reluctantly pulled them off the shelf and went to iron them. When Harold walked by and saw me ironing them, with eyebrows raised he asked, "Are you wearing those today?" I muttered yes. I did not want to be asked any more questions.

As Harold went to finish getting ready for church, I quickly grabbed the cordless phone, bolted back to the laundry room, and shut the door behind me. I called my spiritual mentor Rhonda for encouragement. She had been discipling me and teaching me about the gifts of the Holy Spirit and our responsibility to the gospel. I told her what I had heard from the Holy Spirit about wearing camouflage pants. She was very excited to see what God was up to. Through a nervous smile, I reminded her that it was not her whom the Lord instructed to wear army fatigues to church!

I walked back to my closet to find my dressy brown sweater and high heel brown leather boots. I was doing everything I could to tone down those pants. It didn't work.

On the way to church, I kept telling the Lord that I didn't know what he was up to, but whatever it was I did not want to do it. In spite of that conversation, the instructions I received from him were to not visit with folks when I arrive at the church, but to go straight to the pastor's office and speak to the lady who is always there in the morning before services.

As I walked through the front door, the stares and comments commenced. Let me just tell you, this is a rural church in Louisiana, a hunter's paradise, so I don't know what the big deal was about the pants!

I made no eye contact as I walked swiftly and stealthily to the office. I was accustomed to spending time in the pastor's office as the lady there and I were the two who kept the accounting books for the church. She was a sweet woman with a friendly, encouraging demeanor. When I walked inside, I shared with her that I felt the Lord was up to something and that I didn't know what it was. She looked at me and smiled real big, saying, "Honey, you just be obedient." I can still hear her words today.

I ducked out of the office and by now, I feel that I am in this tunnel type of vision. All I can see is what is right in front of me as I follow the Holy Spirit's leading. Everything else was blurry around me. Making my way down the hallway toward the sanctuary, I turned left instead of the normal right. There I observed a couple entering a side door who hardly ever attended this church. I continued to say to the Lord that I didn't know what he was up to, but that we could not do what he had planned today because this couple was here. I did not want to ruin their occasional attendance at services on this day. Now, let's just stop and think about this. Here I am telling God that he can't do something. A little arrogant, I know. He gently told me that his plan was not about them.

As I made my way to our seats in the front row, Harold pulled me aside to introduce me to a local business owner who had never been to church here before. Harold knew this man from his former life, that is before I became his wife. Well don't you know this gentleman looked me up and down. You can just imagine his expression when he saw the pants! I simply smiled and continued to my seat while repeating to the Lord what I had said earlier. His answer was the same.

The service started as the five-person choir, worship leader, pianist and drummer led the congregation in contemporary songs. But I wasn't singing. Instead, tears flowed from my eyes down my cheeks. My body launched into a shaking-uncontrollably, snot-laden type of cry. And I'm not a crier! I could not contain the tears! I realized later I was releasing all the fear that had been building up in me to that point.

Harold turned and asked me what was wrong, but I could not tell him because I didn't know. Still, I was sure that the Lord wanted to do something through me because of the vision I had in the morning before church, but I had no clue how it would play out.

We sat down as the singing continued. My spiritual mentor Rhonda, who is usually late and sits in the back of the church, walked to the front and sat down in the section opposite me. I made a mental note of her doing this because it was unusual. I told the Lord that he would have to tell me exactly what to do because I did not know what he wanted.

With the congregation still singing, Rhonda got up from her front row seat and walked the few paces to the side of the platform and knelt down to pray. The Holy Spirit spoke to me just then and said, "You must decrease so that I can increase. Go get down by her on the altar." I did not know at the time that he just quoted a scripture. I obeyed and knelt down beside Rhonda. With eyes closed, I too began to pray. I sensed a woman kneel next to me, but because my eyes were shut I didn't know who it was at the time. I found out later it was the worship leader who felt an unction from the Holy Spirit to step down from her spot on the platform and join us on our knees. Just then, a woman from the congregation sensing the need to pray got up from her seat and knelt on the other side of Rhonda.

Under the direction of the Holy Spirit I began to speak quietly commanding the spirits that they had to leave. I began binding and loosing as the scripture commands us to, but again was not aware of this particular verse. When I was done, the woman next to me immediately got up and left.

As the music continued on, the Lord told me to step up on the platform and go pray for a particular woman in the choir. Turns out it was the woman who was separated from her husband.

I walked up beside her, my back to the congregation, and gently pushed her microphone down from her face while covering it. I then began to pray for her. The Lord had me command the spirit that was oppressing her to leave. I hugged her and she wept.

I then turned to my left and saw a demon staring at me through this young woman who was singing in the choir. Mind you, I'm still in this tunnel vision only seeing what's in front of me. I didn't see a physical demon but I knew one was there in the spiritual realm and it was staring at me. I commanded aloud that "I see you and to leave the girl." At that very moment, the girl ran off the stage and back to her seat.

With my backside still facing the congregation, the Lord directed me to call the separated woman's husband up to the platform. So, I turned around and at just that moment, the singing stopped but the pianist kept playing. I can only see the husband, no one else. I called his name loud enough for him to hear me telling him that the Lord wanted him to come up there. He shook his head no.

In the next moment, my eyes went to another man to the right whom I could make out in the tunnel vision. His arms were folded and the Holy Spirit told me that this is the spirit of arrogance and to move on.

The Holy Spirit instructed me to call on the husband again. By this time, Harold had stood up and walked behind the man's seat and was encouraging him to get up. The Lord had me call the husband one more time, but he still refused to come up to the stage. As I looked over the congregation I saw the pastor. The Holy Spirit told me, "That is a spirit of deception, tell it to leave." I obeyed by speaking that out in my normal voice and commanding it to go.

It's important to point out that what was going on was very orderly as the Holy Spirit took over. God is not the author of confusion (1 Corinthians 14:33).

I then observed a woman standing against the back wall. It was the same angry woman who came to my house in one of my previous testimonies. The Holy Spirit told me that there was a spirit of witchcraft on her. He said to tell it to get off. I obeyed, but when I made eye contact, her eyes grew large and were full of fear and panic.

At this point, the Holy Spirit told me I could sit down. As I wearily stepped off the platform, Harold stood up by his seat and explained some of what just took place by educating our fellow parishioners on the gifts of the Holy Spirit operating in the body of the church (1 Corinthians 12:4-7).

Sensing a stirring of the Spirit, or manifestation of the Spirit (1 Corinthians 12:7), the drummer felt directed to get up from behind his drum set, walk to the third row back in the congregation and pray for a man's healing of arthritis. This man hardly ever attends church but happened to be there that day.

Collapsing in my seat, the Holy Spirit told me that his strength is perfected in my weakness, another quote from scripture that I did not know at the time. My assignment was not finished though. The Holy Spirit instructed me to get up and minister to the young woman who had run off the stage, as well as the angry woman in the back covered in witchcraft. Before I made my way to each of the two women, Rhonda was already there loving on both of them. Rhonda is a strong woman of God who regularly hears from the Lord. By the time I walked over to the angry woman against the back wall, her whole countenance had changed. Her guard was let down and she was receptive to my prayers and comforting.

As Rhonda and I were praying privately with those ladies, a male attendee stood up by his seat, walked into the aisle and began prophesying words of edification over the congregation.

The music stopped, and the man went back to his seat. The preacher now stepped up to the pulpit to deliver his message. To this day, I don't recall what all he said, but I do remember he was angry. As I listened, I heard this gurgling voice say, "I'm the big one and I've got your pastor." I heard this in my born-again spirit.

I was very uncomfortable in that moment, so I got up from my seat and walked to the pastor's office. Exhausted, but still feeling the presence of the Holy Spirit, I asked emphatically "Lord, what was that?" Just then, a woman joined me in the office exclaiming, "That was God!" She laughed and said, "He used you of all people! You're usually so quiet." I responded, "Yeah, doesn't he have a sense of humor." Turns out, this was the woman who knelt down next to Rhonda on the side of the platform to pray. She's an excitable person on fire for the Lord who loves to share her passion for Jesus with others. I trusted her discernment in that moment.

That evening, I told the Lord that he was going to have to give me words to say when people asked me what had happened. He said, "Tell them that I spoke to and through those who would receive me." I tear up still today just remembering his voice when he gave me that answer. I asked the Lord why he had me wear the camouflage pants and he gave me this verse:

> *Thou therefore endure hardness, as a good soldier of*
> *Jesus Christ.* (2 Timothy 2:3)

Let me share with you the fruit that came as a result of being obedient to the Holy Spirit's leading that morning. Mind you, I wasn't aware of some of this until months later and sadly, no one came forth in the church to testify of what they received. The man who never came to church was healed of arthritis on that day he chose to be there. The separated wife who was singing in the choir said she felt like a ten-pound object left out of her back. She had been playing some occult game in her search for answers in her life's struggles. She and her husband reunited. The young woman in the choir had a falling out with her best friend who was sitting in the church that day and their friendship was restored.

As the Lord reminds us in his word, persecution will follow and indeed it did with us at this church after this profound and revealing manifestation of the Holy Spirit. The pastor, who was one of Harold's longtime friends, accused him and I of staging the whole incident. We were told that we had an evil spirit among us. Harold and the pastor are no longer friends. The man with the spirit of arrogance said that "God wouldn't use a woman to do what had happened," that is, operate in the gifts of discernment. Most of the people in the church who didn't understand what took place that Sunday avoided me. Again, God warns us of this in Hosea 4:6.

Harold was told he could no longer share, teach, or preach in the pulpit. He ended up resigning from the elder body, and we moved to the back row of the church. We were there about a year after that Sunday until God released us from that church.

Now that I know more about the gifts of the Spirit and the order of operations in the church body assembly, that stirring up of the Spirit was perfectly orchestrated by the Holy Spirit that morning. Members of the church had been begging God to open up the windows of heaven and pour out his anointing. But when the Holy Spirit showed up, most missed him. He was there to set the captives free, to heal, and to restore—all the things Jesus did when he was here.

Jesus' Spirit now lives in us to accomplish his will. He works through willing vessels, like I was that morning, who are totally submitted to him. I love being part of setting others free. Over the years, I have gotten better about not fearing man and man's opinion. This is what the Lord says about it:

> *The fear of man bringeth a snare: but whoso putteth his trust in the Lord shall be safe.* (Proverbs 29:25)

> *For God hath not given us the spirit of fear; but of power, and of love, and of a sound mind.* (2 Timothy 1:7)

What is interesting to me, in my observation of church-going people who believe in the gifts of the Spirit, is that they like them all except the discerning of spirits (1 Corinthians 12:8-10). Folks are good with the prophesying, words of wisdom and knowledge, and healing, but leave the "casting out of devils" alone (Mark 16:17). When you read what Jesus did, this appeared to be a daily activity. It wasn't a big deal to him. He recognized these evil spirits and told them to leave. As a result, people were set free. God's government invaded the situation and darkness left.

People are still in bondage. There are still demonic spirits, and Jesus is who he always was and still is. Hebrews 13:8 tell us, *"Jesus Christ the same yesterday, and to day, and for ever."* He now lives in all born-again believers with a desire to set people free. It is just so clear and simple to me what our roles are as good soldiers of Jesus Christ. May you have a revelation of who he is in you as well as you continue on in this journey.

APPLICATION ASSIGNMENT

1. Sow Proverbs 28:1 in your heart. Remember, you already have the boldness according to this scripture.

2. Ask the Lord in your prayer time for one person he wants you to pray with face to face. Some of you are already comfortable doing this, while others of you may not be. If you regularly step out and pray for people, then ask the Lord for a word of knowledge and then give it to the person. If it's your first time, continue to sow the boldness spoken of in Proverbs 28:1 into your heart and then step out. It's time to be a doer of the word!

3. Journal your journey.

CHAPTER 10

YOUR PART: LIVING A LIFE OF DOMINION, HOW GREAT IT IS

L et me begin this with emphatically stating, we do not have dominion over people. That would be called witchcraft. However, let's look at what God says about dominion in Genesis 1:28:

> *And God blessed them, and God said unto them, Be fruitful, and multiply, and replenish the earth, and* **subdue it***: and* **have dominion** *over the fish of the sea, and over the fowl of the air, and over every living thing that moveth upon the earth. (emphasis added)*

Do you remember the scripture that God will not alter or change what he has already spoken (Psalms 89:34)? His word is forever settled in heaven (Psalms 119:89). He can't change his word because Jesus is the word. Jesus Christ is the same yesterday, today, and forever (Hebrews 13:8). There are many scriptures that bare witness to this truth regarding God's word.

This would be a really good time for you to stop and ask the Holy Spirit for revelation and guidance into these truths. The carnal part of you is going to tend to reject the things that I share. That is perfectly fine, but I'm going to move on believing that he wants me to tell you about these amazing, powerful truths. I want to share one of my favorite quotes and it is by early twentieth-century evangelist Smith Wigglesworth:

> *God has privileged us in Christ Jesus to live above the ordinary human plane of life. Those who want to be ordinary and live on a lower plane can do so, but as for me, I will not.*

I love it! Look what my Lord said:

> *Verily, verily, I say unto you, He that believeth on me, the works that I do shall he do also; and greater works than these shall he do; because I go unto my Father.* (John 14:12)

If we are told to subdue and have dominion over the things in the earth, what does that look like? The word subdue, according to Strong's Concordance, means to "tread down, to conquer, bring into subjection." The word dominion means to "reign, rule, overtake." Have you read the story of Jonah from the viewpoint of having dominion over the fish of the sea? I have, and I want you to see this:

> *And the Lord **spake** unto the fish, and it vomited out Jonah upon the dry land.* (Jonah 2:10 emphasis added)

Do you see that the Lord "spoke" to the fish? The fish obeyed. If the fish had been in 15,000 feet of water and just spit him out, Jonah would have drowned and never made it to his assignment in Nineveh. Yes, it was the Lord speaking to the fish, but he gave us dominion also. Go back and read Genesis 1:28.

At this moment regarding these scriptures, what kind of soil (from the parable in Mark 4) would you say best describes the condition of your heart? Only you know where you are when it comes to receiving these scriptures. Look how Paul describes this dominion using the name of Jesus:

> *Wherefore God also hath highly exalted him, and given him a name which is **above every name**: that at the*

*name of Jesus every knee should bow, of **things** in heaven, and **things in earth**, and **things** under the earth.* (Philippians 2:9-10 emphasis added)

Whatever thing has a name has to submit to the name of Jesus!

TESTIMONIES OF APPLYING GOD'S WORD

I have many testimonies in this category because I live in the country and have animals. This first testimony, though, involves my son, TC.

Between the ages of three and five, my son was not allowed to eat hard candy. There were several occasions when hard candy got stuck in his throat, so it was off limits.

One afternoon, we stopped at Harold's office for a visit. We left the office, and I was driving down a two-lane road with no shoulders. I was talking to TC who was in a booster seat in the back. When I asked him a question, he didn't respond. I turned around to see him lifting himself up and out of his seat, unable to breath. He was not gasping for air and he was not choking, but there was no sound coming from him.

Fear tried to grip my heart as I looked for a place to pull over on this narrow road. I did not know CPR. From down deep in my spirit, I yelled with a voice of authority, "In the name of Jesus, loose from him!" As I pulled into a parking lot, that piece of candy shot out of his mouth and he caught it in his hand. I rushed out of the truck and went to him in the back seat. He was crying and telling me how sorry he was for eating the candy that someone gave to him at Harold's office. All I could do was hug him and thank Jesus.

So, what happened? I had been meditating on the dominion scriptures and the name of Jesus Christ. I had read this scripture a few days before:

And I will give unto thee the keys of the kingdom of heaven: and whatsoever thou shalt bind on earth shall be bound in heaven: and whatsoever thou shalt loose on earth shall be loosed in heaven. (Matthew 16:19)

This scripture was not in my heart yet. The word "loose" was not in my normal everyday vocabulary. However, the Holy Spirit brought it back to my remembrance in that moment. I had a choice in those few seconds. I could allow fear to control me, or I could believe the word of God and use my authority over that "thing" called candy.

Do you see the power that is in the word when you believe it and act on it? Isn't it awesome? Isn't he awesome? I'm telling you, God's sovereignty is so incredible in the way that he intended for us to live in his kingdom on the earth as it is in heaven. He even had this intention with the children of Israel regarding doing his word:

> *And ye shall teach them your children, speaking of them when thou sittest in thine house, and when thou walkest by the way, when thou liest down, and when thou risest up. And thou shalt write them upon the door posts of thine house, and upon thy gates: that your days may be multiplied, and the days of your children, in the land which the Lord sware unto your fathers to give them, **as the days of heaven upon the earth.*** (Deuteronomy 11:19-21 emphasis added)

At my place out in the country, we have cows including a bull, and because of the proximity of our property with the neighbor, we run all of our cows together. One day, my son and I were in the pasture headed to the woods to look for my husband. All of a sudden, my son grabbed the back of my arms and yelled. I turned around to see one of the neighbor's cows charging us. My heart leapt into my throat, and in that moment Genesis 1:26 came flooding in. All I heard was, "Dominion over the cattle of the field." I pointed my finger at the charging cow and yelled, "Suzy, in the name of Jesus, you stop!" (Yes, the cow's name is Suzy.) She stopped in her tracks blowing and snorting. She had a calf a few days before and her instinct was to protect, however we weren't near her calf.

I told her that we were not going to bother her calf and to turn around and go to it. Do you know what she did? She turned around and went to her calf. I turned to my son and said, "That's how you do it." My heart rate was contrary to the boldness that I was experiencing though in that moment of dominion and victory.

Several years ago, there was a red-tailed hawk in our yard that built a nest and had three babies. A windstorm came through and blew the nest apart. Harold found two of the babies on the ground. He built a platform as tall as the ladder would allow placing it near the tree that held the remains of the nest. He put the two babies on the platform.

The next day there was only the smallest of the two baby hawks left on the platform. The other baby was back in the nest. For weeks we would lay thawed deer meat out on the platform for the eyas to eat. We named him Freedom.

It was drawing near to the time that we would be leaving for a planned trip to Colorado. We questioned what we should do with him. I remembered Genesis 1:26, dominion over the fowl of the air. I stood at the fence and spoke to the mama hawk (I didn't see her, I just spoke it out) that the eyas on the platform was her responsibility. I explained that we could not teach it to hunt and that she needed to come and feed him, in the name of Jesus. I went inside.

An hour or so later, I returned to see what was going on with the platform outside. I watched as the mama hawk flew in and dropped a snake on that platform. Thank you, Jesus! The day we were leaving, we watched Freedom fly off for the first time. About a year later, a hawk landed on the lowest branch of an oak tree right outside our front door. I walked out and he just sat there watching me. I hollered for Harold to come and see. The hawk stayed on that branch as we admired his beauty. We believed that it was Freedom.

Living life with dominion has totally changed the way we handle situations, including the words that we speak and the humility we feel. We are acting God's way, which is in accordance with his kingdom principles.

APPLICATION ASSIGNMENT

1. Ask the Holy Spirit to reveal these truths to you. Read Genesis 1:26-28 with the understanding that God has not altered these words that came out of his mouth.

2. Do you think a mosquito ever bit Jesus? I asked my son this when he was younger, and his response was as mine was, no. I began the war on mosquitoes with my authority. They were disobedient in the beginning but began to yield to the name of Jesus. Ask the Holy Spirit to reveal to you something that is coming against you. Remember, every name must bow its knee. Use your authority to stop it.

3. Journal your experience.

CHAPTER 11

YOUR PART: YOU MEAN
I HAVE WHAT I SAY?

We live in a world where people don't say what they mean or mean what they say. They spend thousands of dollars in legal fees trying to take back what was said by way of retractions and apologies that aren't sincere. There is a war on words from political correctness to evil rhetoric dominating the way we communicate.

I totally believe in and support the Constitution of the United States of America. In fact, let me just include the First Amendment for you to read:

> *Congress shall make no law respecting an establishment of religion, or prohibiting the free exercise thereof; or abridging the freedom of speech, or of the press; or the right of the people peaceably to assemble, and to petition the Government for a redress of grievances. (Restoring the Constitution Handbook,* http://www.FreedomWorks.org)

This is the law of the land. This is what God says about the law of man:

> *Submit yourselves to every ordinance of man for the Lord's*
> *sake...*(1 Peter 2:13)

As believers in Jesus Christ, what does God's government say about the words that should be coming out of our mouths? First let's examine who we are in Christ, our identity, before we address our speech.

We are his ambassadors representing his government on the earth (2 Corinthians 5:20). He has made us kings and priests (Revelation 1:6.) He has given us dominion and authority over things. We are created in his image and he created everything by his spoken word (Hebrews 1:3). It is no longer us that lives, but Christ is in us (Galatians 2:20). He is the word (John 1:1, 1:14)!

Now, let's look at several admonitions to us regarding our speech:

> *Let no corrupt communication proceed out of your mouth,*
> *but that which is good to the use of **edifying**, that it may*
> *minister **grace unto the bearers**. And grieve not the*
> *holy Spirit of God, whereby ye are sealed unto the day of*
> *redemption. Let all bitterness, and wrath, and anger, and*
> *clamour, and **evil speaking**, be put away from you...*
> (Ephesians 4:29-31 emphasis added)
>
> *Let your speech be always with grace, seasoned with salt,*
> *that ye may know how ye ought to answer every man.*
> (Colossians 4:6)
>
> *Therewith bless we God, even the Father; and therewith*
> *curse we men, which are made after the similitude of*
> *God. Out of the same mouth proceedeth blessing and*
> *cursing. My brethren, these things ought not so to be.*
> (James 3:9-10)

Do you see what God's kingdom says about our speech? We must line up our lives with the kingdom of God. It is so important that you plant the word in your heart. Jesus said that out of the abundance of the heart the mouth speaks (Matthew 12:34). He also said that it's not what goes in the mouth that defiles a man, but what comes out of his mouth (Matthew 15:11). As one listens to your words, what is coming out is evidence of what is in your heart.

Death and life are contained in the power of our tongue (Proverbs 18:21). The cause and effect principle begins when words are released from our mouths. There is either life or death that results from the words released. Solomon goes on to say in Proverbs 18:21 that you will eat the fruit from those words spoken. The book of Proverbs is full of wisdom and instruction on the power that your tongue has the capacity to release. What about when you come into agreement with others with words, whether good or bad:

> *This is the third time I am coming to you. In the mouth of*
> *two or three witnesses shall **every word** be established.*
> (2 Corinthians 13:1 emphasis added)

Every word that goes out of our mouth is a seed. This seed will produce good fruit or bad fruit. Every seed produces after its own kind. Go back and read Genesis 1:11-12. Whatever you sow, you will reap (Galatians 6:7). God's word is the incorruptible seed (1 Peter 1:23); it is spirit and life (John 6:63). If you want life, you must speak life. When you believe what God says, that is faith. Faith speaks.

> *We having the same spirit of faith, according as it is written,*
> ***I believed**, and therefore have **I spoken; we also believe**,*
> *and therefore **speak**;* (2 Corinthians 4:13 emphasis added)

What are you speaking? What do you believe? Whatever you believe is what is coming out of your mouth. Faith speaks what God says. However, you have to believe what God says, and when you do, you say what God says.

When you believe that you can have what God says, look at how Jesus said this would work:

> *For verily I say unto you, that whosoever **shall say** unto this*
> *mountain, Be thou removed, and be thou cast into the sea;*
> *and shall **not doubt in his heart, but shall believe** those*
> *things which **he saith** shall come to pass; he shall have*
> *whatsoever he saith. Therefore I say unto you, what things*
> *soever ye desire, when ye pray, **believe** that ye receive them,*
> *and ye shall have them.* (Mark 11:23-24 emphasis added)

Everything in God's kingdom works in this same way. It is no different than how you received salvation. I called to share with them what I had prayed so they would have confirmation on what they heard from the Lord.

One of the key points in Mark 11 is that you believed you received when you prayed. We walk by faith and not by sight (2 Corinthians 5:7). Jesus told Thomas that the ones who believed and did not see were blessed. All things begin in seed form in the natural and in the kingdom of God. Go back to Mark 4 and review this amazing parable that Jesus taught.

TESTIMONY OF APPLYING THE WORD

Speaking God's word continues to be a growing part of my life. I read his word; pray his word; confess his word; dream about his word; and teach others about his word. It has become the priority in my life. I have experienced so much fruit from eating his word. I'll share a testimony of how I took the word and prayed the word believing that I received when I prayed.

Harold led a weekly Bible study and over time attendance grew. We began to have more people who would join us by Skype. We were getting teachings on CDs from a ministry that we supported. With permission, I would copy the CDs and give them to the attendees who were local, and send by mail to the folks who were not. I had to buy blank CDs, envelopes, and stamps to make all this happen, but I saw my efforts as part of my personal ministry of "reconciling people to God" (2 Corinthians 5:18).

During my time homeschooling my son, we read a book about George Mueller. He was a man who built and operated an orphanage, trusting God for every single aspect of it. He never asked a single man for money. He went to God for everything and God supplied.

I wanted to trust my Father and attempt this "walking by faith" concept that George Mueller experienced. I used Acts 10:34 and Philippians 4:19 in my conversation with God one morning. He is no respecter of persons, and if my Father did it for George Mueller, he would do it for me. Mind you, I'm sharing the conversation I had with God. I then reminded him that he supplies the needs that I have. I did not ask him for money in this situation. I told God that I needed CDs, envelopes, and stamps. I thanked him for his promises and believed that I received in that moment. I wrote in my journal what I had prayed and when. I never mentioned this to another person, not even my husband.

The following Wednesday night after Bible study, a lady walked up to me and handed me a card. She asked me not to open it until we got home. When we got home, I opened the card and inside it was $300 cash. The note indicated that every month, she and husband would set aside an amount in order to give as God directed (above their tithe). They both prayed, and her husband felt that the Lord told him to give the money to us. I cried with joy because it was an answer to my prayer a few days before. I called to share with them what I had prayed so they would have confirmation on what they heard from the Lord.

In this instance, money was not the issue as I had the funds to buy the items, but I wanted to use this opportunity to step out in faith and trust God for what I needed based on what his word says. Since that incredible experience, my faith has gone way beyond stamps and blank CDs. But I had to start somewhere on this faith journey and move past trusting him just for my salvation. He's so much more!

APPLICATION ASSIGNMENT

1. Choose one small area in which you want to trust God.

2. Find the promise in his word regarding this area.

3. Get that word (seed) into your heart so that you can release it by faith when you pray.

4. When you know that you believe it, go to your Father and talk to him about his word and what you want from him. Believe that you received it when you prayed.

5. Journal the journey.

CHAPTER 12

YOUR PART: THERE IS STILL POWER IN PRAYER

If God is totally in control, why is the word "prayer" and "pray" listed in so many scriptures in the Bible? If he controls all things, why do you pray? With this kind of mindset, no wonder more Christians are not praying because they don't think there is power in their prayers.

To boil it down and keep it simple, prayer to me is just talking with, and/ or singing to my Father. I don't complicate it, rationalize it, or try to explain it. Jesus is my way, my truth, and my life. He made it a reality that I can go directly to my Father because of the blood he shed for me and reconciled me back to the Father (John 14:6, 2 Corinthians 5:18).

If you are reconciled to the Father—which Jesus made possible—why don't you ever go and talk to him. When I speak to God, I know that he hears me because I believe what his word says about it.

> *And this is the confidence that we have in him, that, if we ask any thing according to his will [his word], **he heareth us**: And if we **know** that he hear us, whatsoever we ask,*

*we **know that** we have the petitions that we desired of him.* (1 John 5:14-15 emphasis added)

Do you see the level of confidence that we should be walking in based on what his word says? The principle that most people miss is the fact that we should talk to God based on his word when it comes to petitioning. It is his word that is forever settled in heaven (Psalms 119:89). It is his promises that we need to experience in the natural realm that belong to us (2 Corinthians 1:20). If he has given (past tense) all things that pertain unto life and godliness through the knowledge of him, there shouldn't be very many things that we are "asking" of him (2 Peter 1:3-4). My prayer time is spent mainly worshipping him for who he is, blessing him, thanking him, and then listening to what he wants to talk to me about.

I have a journal beside my bed. Almost every morning, I get on my knees with my head bowed down on the floor with my journal, pen, and flashlight. My husband taught me this. We don't turn on any lights early in the morning. He gets up earlier than I do to spend his quiet time with the Lord. Keeping the lights off and just using the flashlight prevents the outside world from creeping in on the eyes and ears. We have matured to the point that yes, we can still hear him even with the lights on. I don't even come out for coffee until I get my word from my Father. This is how important his voice is to me.

When you begin to sow the word in your heart, you learn that God's word is real and true. It changes how you think and what you say. You begin to think and talk what his word says. This is how I talk to my Father based on his own word. Early on in my walk with the Lord I would ask him for wisdom and strategy (James 1:5, James 4:7). As I grew spiritually based on the word, I discovered there is a more direct way to obtain the wisdom that God has already provided. It's through what's called praying in the spirit. When I do this, I am praying the wisdom of God, my spirit to his Spirit. (1 Corinthians 14:2, 1 Corinthians 2:7). I'll share more on this in a later chapter.

I'm taking a short detour here. Harold and I often have people ask us to pray for them to have wisdom. These are not "babes in Christ" either. Now look, I'm not opposed to praying for Christians; we do it all the time. But God says for you to ask him for it. It's time for Christians to stand up and take their place; get in God's word for themselves; believe it, and act on it.

There needs to be some maturing that takes place in the body of Christ. It's time that you get off the bottle and start feasting on the filet mignon. Even cows stop drinking milk! My husband says this is the reason he doesn't drink milk. Have you ever seen a nine-month-old calf trying to nurse? The calf nearly has to bend down on its knees to get anything. Isn't that a funny picture? If the calf could, it would stay on the milk unless it was pulled from the mama cow.

It's time to move from milk to meat. It's time to do the word. This is how Jesus described it:

> *Jesus saith unto them, My **meat** is to **do the will** of him*
> *that sent me, and to **finish his work**.*
> (John 4:34 emphasis added)

Christ is in you and there is still work to do as long as people are lost and in darkness.

There is a time for talking to our Father and there is a time that we should be declaring his word in situations. As a king (Revelation 1:6), you should be decreeing the word of God. Why?

> *Thou shalt also decree a thing, and **it shall** be established*
> *unto thee: and the light shall shine upon thy ways.*
> (Job 22:28 emphasis added)

Jesus is our King of kings (Revelation 19:16). He tells us in Job 22:28 that you are to decree a thing. What is that thing that you want established? This scripture says that it will be established to you. Who is the light that will shine on your ways?

> *This then is the message which we have heard of him,*
> *and declare unto you, that **God is light**, and in him is no*
> *darkness at all. (1 John 1:5 emphasis added)*

Speak what God says and you will get what God says to the degree that you believe what God says. In God's sovereignty, he is the one who decided he would make you a king to declare his word on the earth as it is in heaven. He also decided that he would make you an ambassador for Christ (2 Corinthians 5:20).

Here's how the dictionary describes what an ambassador is: *A minister of the highest rank employed by one prince or state, at the court of another, to manage the public concerns of his own prince or state, and* **representing the power and dignity of his sovereign**. *Ambassadors are ordinary, when they reside permanently at a foreign court; or* **extraordinary**, *when they are sent on a special occasion...* (Webster's Dictionary 1828 - Online Edition, s.v. "ambassador," accessed August 20, 2018, http://webstersdictionary1828.com/ Dictionary/ambassador)

Notice that Paul said in 2 Corinthians that we are ambassadors for Christ. It is Christ who is the anointed One. We are on special assignment and this is not our home (1 Peter 2:11, Philippians 3:20, Ephesians 2:6). As an ambassador representing God's government on the earth, we must know his law and principles. It is for us to speak what he says in every situation that is contrary to his kingdom.

Are you beginning to see your different roles in communicating God's will? We have a part to play in his will being done on earth as it is in heaven. He has chosen to work and speak through mankind from the beginning. It started when he gave man dominion and told Adam to name the animals (Genesis 1:26, Genesis 2:19). In God's sovereignty, this is how he chose to operate. God needs us to accept his way of doing things, and cooperate with his will, which is his word. I continue to humble myself (it is a daily process), and I choose to believe what he says because I love him.

TESTIMONIES OF APPLYING GOD'S WORD

Remember, this is a process of seed, time, and harvest (Genesis 8:22, Mark 4:11-20, 28-29). I continue to sow, learn, and grow, and I enjoy the process that God established. The application of this kingdom principle is used in everyday living, even in simple examples like what happens on my farm.

Right after one of our cows calved, she walked away from it without it nursing. This is a huge no-no. Harold was unable to deal with the situation right then as he had to leave for an appointment in town to minister with someone. He said that he would deal with the calf when he got home. He told me to keep on eye on the calf so that the buzzards would not come and peck its eyes out and kill it. (I know, graphic but true.)

I poured a cup of coffee, grabbed a bucket to sit on, and placed my cell phone nearby. I was not happy. I had many things to accomplish that morning, and this was not on my schedule. As I sat there, the buzzards began to gather in the trees in the pasture. One landed in the tree close to where I was perched on the bucket. The Holy Spirit brought back to my remembrance, "dominion over the fowl of the air" (Genesis 1:26). See, that is how he speaks to me on the inside in that still, quiet voice. As I looked at that ugly buzzard eyeing my calf, power rose up on the inside of me. Courage began to swell too. I stood up and pointed my finger and told the buzzard that this calf was mine and not his. I commanded him to leave the area in the name of Jesus Christ and to not return. As I talked, he looked defiant, but listened. After I used the name of Jesus Christ, he and the rest of his flock flew away.

Can I just say, it is so awesome to live life this way! Now, there was still something on me, or should I say stirring about in my soul. I sat back down on that bucket feeling not quite right to get up and leave just yet. I happened to call my sister to share with her what was going on with my morning. She proceeded to point out to me that I was in fear. Well, after what I just experienced with the buzzards leaving, I doubted her assertion. She proceeded to ask me why then was I still sitting on the bucket. You know what? She was right and I told her so. She explained that if I believed what I said about the buzzards not returning, I would go in the house and get my things done. So, I gathered up my bucket and coffee and went inside the house. Later that day, Harold returned home, and that mama cow ended up nursing her calf. That calf ended up being a blessing to us in many ways.

As an ambassador of God's kingdom on the earth, I represent what God says, but I have to believe what he says, say it, and act on it. In my responsibility as his ambassador, God has called me to have the authority to release his power, his word, out of my mouth into situations that are contrary to his government on the earth, which is his kingdom that I represent.

I've mentioned several things already regarding a mission trip I took to Haiti. It was filled with so many God moments, and it was such good training ground for me in applying the word and hearing the Holy Spirit. My team and I were installing water systems (two five-gallon buckets with a filter), in addition to providing medical assistance, prayer, and worship time. As we sat in the community center, my eyes were drawn to a petite elderly woman in a cotton gown with a straw hat on her head. She was so adorable. As the mission team demonstrated how the filters worked, she dozed off. When the meeting was over, she woke up. As she walked off, I noticed that she was bent over.

As we trudged through the rice fields to the various houses in this particular community, I saw that same woman bathing in the canal with the cows. The canal water is what's used for the community's drinking supply. The woman caught my glance and waved at me. I waved back. Later, as our five-person team was approaching the last house to install the water systems, guess who walks up? Yes, that precious woman I had seen twice that day.

The team and I rotated who would explain, demonstrate, and set up the water system and then who would minister. It was my time to minister. Imagine that! This woman, in her native Creole language, instructed a young man to bring us two chairs, and then through a translator communicated to me that she needed to go and put on her underpants and that she would be right back. (Remember she had just bathed in the canal.) I noticed again how bent over she was as she walked, yet in spite of her crippling physical stature she was filled with such joy.

When she returned, we made small talk and then I asked if I could pray for her back. I explained that Jesus paid for her right to be healed. She told me that she had been to the voodoo priests for years, but they had not helped her. I followed up by asking if I could put my hand on her, and she said yes. While I did this, I was withdrawing on the inside to give me time to hear from the Holy Spirit. As I closed my eyes and placed my palm on her back, I started to weep. I didn't say a word. Tears just welled up in my eyes and began streaming down my face. All of a sudden, I heard a popping sound. I opened my eyes and looked at her. She stared at me with as much shock on her face as I must have had on mine.

I told the translator to ask her to stand up. She got up from her chair stretching her body upright. She lifted her hands over her head and began to rejoice. Oh my! What an experience. Joy unspeakable! She then uttered the most incredible, endearing words over me. I sobbed again. I asked her if she knew Jesus. Of course, she did. I really didn't have to ask. I knew. As I write this, I feel the stirring of the Holy Spirit. See, he's the same Spirit who was in Jesus, and who is in all believers. Incredible!

I knew what God said about her healing. I knew what Jesus did for us when he was beaten. I knew what he did for my son's heart. I knew that God was no respecter of persons. As his ambassador, king, soldier, and son, I had to release my faith (believe his word), and that precious woman was loosed from that spirit of infirmity that had bound her for years. I didn't command anything to leave nor did I speak a word. See, this is when you have to be one with his Spirit. He will guide you in every situation. Press in to him and learn from him.

There is power in your conversations with our Father. There is power in your worship with him. There is power in the words that come out of your mouth. There is power in believing that you have what you say when you say it. He is that power. His words are power. Jesus is the word (John 1:14).

APPLICATION ASSIGNMENT

1. Keep a journal and pen beside your bed. You can try the flashlight method too.

2. Spend one week getting down on your knees and face before the Lord. Do not ask him for a single thing. Do not complain to him about a single situation. Go to him with thanksgiving in your heart and on your lips.

3. With journal open and pen in hand, ask him to speak to you. Desire to hear his voice. With confidence and expectancy, begin to write the thoughts that you immediately sense. As you write, keep writing. He always wants to talk to you.

4. Thank him and tell him that you love him. I always blow kisses to him when I'm finished, but that's just me. I'm just sharing my relationship with him.

5. Don't go back and read anything that you have written during that week. Let a few days go by and then go back and read what you wrote. It's so lovely.

6. Enjoy your relationship and new prayer time!

CHAPTER 13

YOUR PART: THE PURSUIT OF HEARING GOD'S VOICE

A common question that Harold and I get as we begin to disciple believers is, "How do I know if it's God's voice or it's just me and my thoughts?" I surmise that we have all thought or asked this same type of question in our quest for hearing the Lord. As I began to pursue him through his word, I started to recognize his voice more clearly. Now, let me just admit right now that I don't always hear him in a timely manner. It is not because he isn't speaking to me at the precise moment that I need to hear him. It's that I'm just not listening.

It is so vital to our Christian walk that we know his voice based on his word. So, when you know the scriptures, how can you be sure that it is his voice you're hearing?

> *In the beginning was the Word, and the Word was with God, and the Word was God. The same was in the beginning with God.* (John 1:1-2)

*And the Word was made flesh, and dwelt among us, (and
we beheld his glory, the glory as of **the only begotten** of the
Father,) full of grace and truth.* (John 1:14 emphasis added)

We know that in John 3:16, God sent his only begotten Son. Jesus is the word.
As we learn his word, we learn about him and we can recognize his voice based
on his word. His word promises that it is life. As you ruminate on the word of
God—I like to picture a cow chewing its cud—the word is nourishing and life.
Let me show you how the word has been described in several scriptures:

*It is the spirit that quickeneth; the flesh profiteth nothing:
the **words** that I speak unto you, **they are spirit**, and
they are life.* (John 6:63 emphasis added)

*For the **word of God is living and active and full of
power** [making it operative, energizing, and effective]. It is
sharper than any two-edged sword, penetrating as far as
the division of the soul and spirit [the completeness of a
person], and of both joints and marrow [the deepest parts
of our nature], exposing and judging the very thoughts and
intentions of the heart.* (Hebrews 4:12 AMP emphasis added)

*My son, attend to my **words**; incline thine ear unto my
sayings. Let them not depart from thine eyes; keep them in
the midst of thine heart. For **they are life** unto those that
find them, and health to all their flesh.* (Proverbs 4:20-22
emphasis added)

As you read God's word, you are taking in life through your eyes. When you
are listening or speaking the word, life is coming in through your ears. The Holy
Spirit is speaking to you on the inside. Have you ever read a scripture and it's
like the words jumped off of the page? That is the Holy Spirit quickening you. It
is Jesus, the Word. It is that "still small voice" that 1 Kings 19:12 describes.

The best way to describe how one hears the voice of God is that when you do
hear it, you just know that you know you've heard it. Jesus said, *"My sheep hear
my voice, and I know them, and they follow me"* (John 10:27).

For me, the process of hearing God's voice is similar to meeting a person for the first time. As I spend time with this person and get to know him or her, I recognize this person's voice. Of course, now with cell phones and contact lists, when someone calls, you don't have to guess who it is by their voice because the contact name pops up on the cell phone screen. To me, it takes all of the fun, guessing, and embarrassment out of the equation. My, how times have changed!

The more I have learned God's word and have sown the scriptures in my heart, the more the Holy Spirit guides and corrects me using the word. Remember the dream that I had with the word "Numbers" written in the sky? Unpleasant memory there, however the teaching that came from the dream was definitely effective.

One morning as I was walking up and down my driveway praying, I decided that I just wanted to praise and bless my Father. As I passed by our cows, I told them that they were created for God's pleasure and that they belonged to him. Scriptures Revelation 4:11 and Psalms 50:10 were coming to mind as I was looking at the cows and praising the Lord.

As I continued walking, a huge flock of brown cow birds landed in the pasture and trees across the road. Their song was so loud and so amazing. I stopped praising the Lord turning my attention to the birds and just watched and listened. As I did, I said, "Oh Lord, they are praising you!" It says that in Psalms 150:6, which the Lord brought to my remembrance at that very moment.

Immediately after, I heard in my born-again spirit the Lord responding to me with, "No, I am rejoicing over you with singing." Oh, how sweet the sound of his voice. Tears welled up in my eyes understanding my Father's precious love for me. I knew that was a scripture in Zephaniah 3:17. It is that love that passes all knowledge that I was experiencing contained in Ephesians 3:19. When the word is in your heart, the fruit of it passes your head knowledge, and it becomes revelation by way of the Holy Spirit and his voice.

Many would describe their relationship and pursuit of hearing God's voice in such varying ways, but I can only explain it based on my own experience. Jesus' description of his words as spirit and life explains why Peter referred to it as an "incorruptible seed" by which we are born again (1 Peter 1:23).

From Genesis to Revelation, there are various ways in which God speaks that are illustrated through the stories in the Bible. One way I seek to hear his voice is by reading his word. The more I venture to hear, the more I hear and grow, and God tells us he loves when we diligently seek him (Hebrews 11:6). Whether it's through a dream, a vision, his creation, or other people, I'm learning to discern his voice based on his word.

TESTIMONIES OF APPLYING GOD'S WORD

Over the years, I have stepped out to practice hearing God's voice. This pursuit reminds me of my son's beagle, Bailey, who would go in the woods to "jump a rabbit." She would sniff through underbrush, run around trees, and investigate holes all in an effort to jump a rabbit. When she would jump that rabbit up, the race was on. The excitement of Bailey's bark is something beyond words, but you get the visual. Don't you think that our Father just loves it when we diligently seek to hear him?

During this journey some years back, a friend of mine's twelve-year-old daughter came to spend a week with us in the summer. I was praying and asking the Lord what he wanted me to teach her and my son while she was here, and he responded with, "I want you to teach them how to hear my voice." I told him that I needed help in that area for myself. I did not feel adequate whatsoever to be teaching on that particular subject. However, I chose to be obedient.

As the week was winding down, I felt that it was time to practice all that we had been learning. I had heard a previous testimony of how these believers would pray for God to give them hints on who he wanted them to minister to, and they would go and look for the person. It sounded like fun to me. So, my son, the girl, and I sat in my truck before leaving the house to go to town. I explained that we were going to pray and ask the Lord who he wanted to minister to today. When I finished praying over what we were about to do, I told them that they were to share with me the first thoughts that came to their mind. I encouraged them that it was the Holy Spirit speaking.

As I was finishing up the prayer with "Amen," my son immediately spouted off his list that he "heard." He said so many things so quickly that I hastily had to find something on which to write them down. Here are the items he heard in his spirit that I listed on the back of a gas receipt: bird, seven, green, yellow, and black panthers. Our little friend said that all she got was boxes. In the moment that I finished the prayer, in my mind I saw a mother and daughter and something was wrong between the two of them.

On our way to the store, I kept telling the Lord that I was trusting him. I was nervous and I wasn't quite sure how it would all play out. He had to listen to me all the way to town, which was about thirty minutes. I'm glad that he is long suffering, aren't you?

As we pulled into the department store parking lot, I had this "feeling" that I should go through a different entrance to the store than I normally do. My son stuffed the gas receipt with the hints into his pants pocket. As we entered the store making our way to the back, there were two women walking in front of us. Our little friend asked me if that was a bird tattoo on her back. I squinted trying to make out the design that was on the lady's shoulder, but I couldn't tell what it was from that far away.

As we ended up near the rear of the store, TC and the girl were asking me if I was going to say anything to the two women we had been following. They were looking to me for answers that I did not have. I stalled by asking them if they were hearing anything from God, and they both responded no.

So, I mustered up the courage to say to the two ladies, "Excuse me." Neither one was looking at us, so they just moved over thinking that we wanted to pass by them. I repeated, "Excuse me." One of the women looked irritably at me and said, "Yes?" I asked if they had a need from the Lord. By the look on her face, I knew I needed to explain myself. I began to tell her how we prayed before we left our house, and God gave us some hints. I commented that my son had gotten a "bird" and that I thought she had a bird tattoo on her back. She pointed her finger to the back of her shoulder and exclaimed, "It's a dove, and I just got it two weeks ago!"

I repeated my question regarding their need, and one of the women said that everyone needs prayer for health. I told her that the prayer need I'm asking about is more specific than that. She then pointed to the woman who was with her saying that she recently had brain surgery to remove a tumor. She continued that they were fearful that the tumor may come back. The woman who had the operation was wearing a wig so I would not have known this just by looking at her. But right then I knew in my born-again spirit that she was the one to whom God wanted to minister.

I asked for the ladies' first names, and they obliged, then excitedly took our hands in order to pray. I prayed like Jesus taught us. They thanked us and we turned to go about our way.

I was convinced with just the bird tattoo on the woman's back that we had accomplished the assignment. However, our little friend asked me if I saw the woman's shirt. I asked my son for the receipt and we walked back over to where they were standing. I asked to look at the shirt that the woman we prayed for was wearing. She was wearing a yellow t-shirt with a green seven, and it had Burgess Elementary under the seven. She said that they were the "black panthers!" Guess where we were standing when we prayed? In front of the shelves holding all of the boxes of games! There were all the hints: bird, seven, green, yellow, and black panthers. The two women started jumping up and down with excitement at this divine appointment, and I was elated to say the least. Look how specific our Father was in order for us to get to the one he wanted to love on.

As I walked off, I kept talking about it and my son responded, "Mom, it's just God." Don't you love that matter-of-fact response? At this point, my grocery list was far from my thoughts, but I did have a few items that needed to be picked up. As we were checking out, I looked behind me and there was the mother and daughter that I saw in my mind. Mom was kind of rough and appeared irritated. The daughter, who seemed about twelve, was very innocent looking, however their countenance showed me there was definitely something going on between them at that moment. I nodded to the kids about who was standing behind me. The Lord then told me to buy the mother and daughter's items. My immediate response was to look in their buggy. You would have done the same thing.

I then proceeded to tell the woman that the Lord wanted me to buy her things. The daughter, who was standing behind her mother, smiled. The mother, visibly offended by my statement, responded in a raspy voice, "I don't need you to buy my things!"

Well, my flesh wanted to kick in and tell her that I didn't want to buy her things. However, I yielded to the Holy Spirit and pressed on. On my third attempt to bless her by buying her things, she surrendered. I paid for all the items in her shopping cart and as I walked off, she said, "Ma'am, thank you." Her whole demeanor and tone had changed. I told her to thank the Lord; that he was the one who did it.

What an incredible journey! How humbling it is to be the Lord's vessel. We have many testimonies of doing this "seeking, listening, and pursuing" assignment. We just need to slow down in the busyness of our mind to tune in to hear him. We have to turn off the television, computer, cell phone and whatever else dominates our attention and thoughts in order to hear him. I don't even want the lights on first thing in the morning so that I can keep my mind stayed on him (Isaiah 26:3). As I have grown in my ability, I can hear God in the midst of all of the distractions, but in the beginning of this journey with the Lord, I wanted to unplug from the world.

Here's another testimony of the effects of hearing God's voice. I was sitting in my truck in a gas station after I had just fueled up, and the Lord told me to buy the woman's gas who was behind me. I was now quite confident of God's voice and so I was waiting for the woman to get out of her truck. I was busy putting my credit card back in my purse and when I looked back, she'd gone into the store. I waited and waited, got impatient, and began to pull out of the gas station. I thought, "Well Lord, I missed you on that one." As I looked back, she was coming out toting a case of beer.

At that point, I was determined to go back and do the Lord's work. To get back to the gas station, I had to head down the road and make a u-turn. As I was driving, I told the Lord that if there's a place beside her at the gas pumps, I would pull in. Sure enough, there was. I pulled in and stepped out of my truck. As I walked over, I asked if she had paid for her gas yet? She looked at me with this puzzled expression. I explained that God wanted me to fill up her tank. She hugged me and thanked me.

As I pumped her gas, I began to tell her that the voice she was hearing was God. I encouraged her to trust his voice. I don't remember all that I said, but she cried. She told me where she worked and to come see her some time. She hugged me again. As I pulled out of the parking lot, I glanced back and saw that she was sobbing, her head buried in her hands. I knew that the Holy Spirit was doing his thing. I thanked him so much for urging me to do the will of the Father.

I shared the testimony with my husband, Harold, so one day, he and a friend had some time to spare so they went to the diner where she worked. They were seated and Harold asked the Holy Spirit which woman it was. The Holy Spirit told him that it was their waitress. So, Harold asked his waitress if a petite blond woman bought her gas recently. She said yes, and asked him to tell me to visit her.

The following week I went to the diner. When I walked in, she came and hugged me. As I sat and drank coffee, she began to share with me that she had been a drug addict for a long time, but had been clean for quite a few years.

She had recently gone out of state to get her three-year-old granddaughter from her son, who was an addict. He was blaming her for the mess he was in, and he kept calling her saying he wanted his daughter back. She began to ask God what to do. She thought that she was hearing him, but she wasn't sure. The very morning she asked God about her situation and what to do was the day I told her that the voice she was hearing was God and to trust him. How wonderful! God is always trying to get the answers to our questions through to us. He wants to throw us a lifeline. In his sovereignty, he has chosen to speak through others who recognize his voice and are obedient to relay the message to those who may question his voice.

To this day, I have maintained a relationship with this precious woman I met at the gas station. It becomes a kingdom connection every time I'm about my Father's business. During this almost twelve-year journey of pressing in to God's word, I still remember names of the strangers for whom I have prayed. There have been many, and in God's kingdom there are no strangers. We are all the family of God, are we not? It has become a reality that in Christ, I live, move, and have my being (Acts 17:28).

APPLICATION ASSIGNMENT

1. Get in your quiet place with your journal and pen.

2. If you are not accustomed to hearing your Father right after you pray, go to him with a "yes or no" type of question.

3. Ask him your question, and then write down the first "thought" that comes to your mind. Trust the answer and then act on it accordingly. (Review Matthew 7:7)

4. If you are more seasoned and want to step out, ask for hints and then go seek out the treasure. Trust the voice of the Holy Spirit.

5. Journal your experience.

CHAPTER 14

YOUR PART: PRAYING IN TONGUES? YES INDEED!

Well, I knew the time was coming that the Lord wanted me to share on the topic of praying in tongues. I did notice though that he waited until the end of the book to include this. See, most readers would have put the book down had I mentioned this subject earlier. Hopefully, based on the word and testimonies under the guidance of the Holy Spirit, you will continue reading.

All that I am going to share with you in this section is what God says are the benefits of praying in an unknown tongue. The matter is between you and the Holy Spirit on what you do with the word (the seed) that is given. Remember, it is the condition of your heart (the ground or soil) as to whether you receive the fruit of this seed or not. He loves you whether you believe or not. If you don't or won't believe, it's OK. But know that without faith, it's impossible to operate in this particular gift.

Remember, it is the Holy Spirit who moved in to your temple when you were born again. All of him moved in. He brought his fruit and his gifts. One of these gifts is referred to as praying or speaking in an "unknown tongue." This is not from the devil, as some would have you think. The Bible is very clear that it is a gift of the Holy Spirit (1 Corinthians 12:4) and that there are two places where it operates: in an assembly of believers, and in your communication with the Lord. I am going to share the benefits to you in your prayer life. These benefits are straight from the word of God. Stop and ask the Holy Spirit to guide you into these truths. He will comfort you and teach you to the degree that you will humble yourself and receive. Ready?

Benefits of Praying in an Unknown Tongue

1. Gives rest and is refreshing to the weary: *For with stammering lips* [remember a baby learns to talk?] *and **another tongue** will he speak to this people. To whom he said, This is the rest wherewith ye may cause the **weary to rest**; and this is the **refreshing**: yet they would not hear.* (Isaiah 28:11-12 emphasis added)

2. Builds you up in your holy faith and keeps you in the love of God: *But ye, beloved, building up yourselves on your most holy faith, **praying in the Holy Ghost**, keep yourselves in the love of God...* (Jude 20-21 emphasis added) This benefit of praying in the Holy Spirit keeps you in God's kind of love when dealing with others and the darkness of this world.

3. As you pray in tongues, you will receive edification. You will be edified. *He that speaketh in an unknown tongue edifieth **himself**...* (1 Corinthians 14:4 emphasis added) Do you remember how David encouraged himself in the Lord when everyone was trying to kill him, and his family and soldiers' families were kidnapped? To make matters worse, all their stuff was stolen and the town was burned down. Read 1 Samuel 30 to see how David stayed encouraged in spite of terrible circumstances. And I thought I had problems! We live in tumultuous times, so it's important you find a way to encourage and edify yourself so you have peace in your life and you stay grounded in the Lord.

How many people do you have in your life who actually encourage you? I don't have very many who do that for me. Most people are so inundated with their own battles, they can't even look up much less encourage someone else. I don't mean to be ugly here, it's just the culture we find ourselves in and what we experience in daily life with people.

4. When you pray in the Spirit, he will pray when you don't know what to pray. He also prays the perfect will of God for you and others.

*Likewise, the Spirit also helpeth our infirmities: for **we know not what we should pray for as we ought**: but the Spirit itself maketh intercession for us with groanings which cannot be uttered. And he that searcheth the hearts knoweth what is the mind of the Spirit, because he maketh intercession for the saints according to the **will of God**.* (Romans 8:26-27 emphasis added). Now see, I just believe what God says in that scripture. Simple. Most of the time, I don't know exactly what to pray, especially when it is about other people and their struggles. But the Holy Spirit knows. He knows everything and he has the answer for everything. Oh, that's right, he is one with the Father, the Creator. In God's sovereignty, he gave us his Spirit who can pray through us as we yield and pray in his language, or another man's language (1 Corinthians 13:1).

5. You pray God's wisdom as you are praying in an unknown tongue. *For he that **speaketh** in an unknown tongue speaketh not unto men, but **unto God**: for no man understandeth him; howbeit in the spirit he **speaketh mysteries**.* (1 Corinthians 14:2 emphasis added)

What are the mysteries that you are speaking?

> But **we speak the wisdom of God in a mystery**, even the
> hidden wisdom, which God ordained before the world unto
> our glory. (1 Corinthians 2:7 emphasis added)

These are the benefits when you pray in the Spirit, also known as praying in tongues. As I write this book I am constantly praying in the Spirit. I need the Holy Spirit's wisdom, not mine, as I convey what the Lord has put on my heart to share with you through the words on these pages.

Praying in tongues is a powerful gift of the Holy Spirit that Satan has managed to distort by deceiving believers to the point that very few experience the power of what God, in his sovereignty, provided for his children. Praying in an unknown tongue is one of the weapons available to you for the spiritual battle in which we all find ourselves.

In 1 Corinthians, Paul listed the order in which this gift should operate in the church, but the enemy has deceived Christians into thinking that this gift has gone away with the passage of time, or that it is of the devil, or that not everyone can do it. More than ever, we need the gifts of the Holy Spirit operating in our lives. All believers who have the indwelling Holy Spirit can pray in tongues. Not all will do so though because they choose not to believe or they are void of knowledge in this area. Here are two examples of God's word not working in a situation:

> Making the **word of God of none effect through your
> tradition**, which ye have delivered: and many such like
> things do ye. (Mark 7:13 emphasis added)

> Then came the disciples to Jesus apart, and said, Why
> could not we cast him out? And Jesus said unto them,
> Because of **your unbelief**.
> (Matthew 17:19-20 emphasis added)

Go ahead, humble yourself and s-t-r-e-t-c-h to believe him! Believe what his word says! If you aren't being stretched to believe for deeper, higher, bigger, better, and more, you aren't walking by faith. Harold says that he feels like pizza dough. Isn't that a great visual? We were not created to be comfortable and to settle down in life. There is a war raging all around, and you have been created to engage, advance, conqueror, and occupy until Jesus, our King, returns.

TESTIMONIES OF APPLYING THE WORD

As I began to learn all the benefits of praying in tongues, I readily jumped on the bandwagon. I was fascinated by the stories of nineteenth and twentieth century men and women whom God used to perform supernatural acts that changed people's lives for the better. Do you know what the common thread was that I discovered among these men and women I read about? They each spent hours praying in tongues. Well, if it worked for them, it would work for me because God said so.

Early on in this journey when I would pray in tongues it seemed foolish to me because I did not comprehend what I was saying. Imagine that! God says in his word that it would be that way. I pressed in and I pressed on in this gift. One evening, as I was preparing for the next day of homeschool, I could not figure out how to work a fifth grade math problem. Yes, you read that correctly. I am a college graduate so I could work it out the way I was taught. However, this particular math curriculum wanted you to work it in several different ways. I took the problem to Harold and asked him to figure it out. He did it the same way I did. I told him that the instructions indicated we couldn't work it that way. He was like me and couldn't figure out another solution.

I decided to quit for the evening and go to bed. As I laid there, I told the Lord that I had a college degree so I should be able to figure this out. As my husband and son will testify, I am somewhat competitive. I don't like to quit. This math problem was one of those times. I began to think about the scripture where Paul says that we have the mind of Christ (1 Corinthians 2:16). I was meditating on the fact that I had the ultimate mathematician living on the inside of me. The Holy Spirit brought the scriptures back to me about praying the wisdom of God when I pray in tongues. So, I began to pray in tongues. All of a sudden, in my mind, I saw that problem worked out on the whiteboard. Do you know that saying, "Hold that thought?" I spoke that very thing out as I jumped out of bed. I went into my classroom, closed the door, turned on the light, and wrote it out on the board. There it was!

See how the word works when you believe him? I have many testimonies in this area, but not enough space to write all of them in this book. Another book? Maybe.

As explained in Romans 8:26-27, the first time that I personally experienced the Holy Spirit interceding for someone else while I was praying in tongues came after I had determined to practice praying for a set amount of time. I was wanting to move from "stammering lips" to the "divers kinds of tongues" (Isaiah 28:11 and 1 Corinthians 12:10). Do you know how I did that? Practice. Yes, practice! People with a religious mindset or a works mindset would disagree with that statement that we need to practice and press in. We have a part to play in stirring up the gifts and fruits of the Holy Spirit. Paul's words were much more eloquent when he said to "covet earnestly."

I was sitting in a rocking chair on the front porch praying in tongues. I prayed and prayed. I looked at my watch and I had only prayed for five minutes. It seemed like a lot longer than that. I continued on. At one point, I saw my friend's ex-husband in my mind. He was in a jail cell, walking towards the bars of the door. He had on a white button-down collared shirt and blue jeans. My friend lives in Dallas and I had not seen her ex-husband in more than ten years. I kept praying in spite of this unusual thought playing out in my mind.

Shortly afterwards, I went in the house and got my cell phone to send my friend a text. I told her I felt like we should pray for her ex-husband. Five minutes later my phone rang. It was my friend. I shared with her that I was praying (I didn't tell her that I was praying in tongues) and that I saw her ex-husband. I explained the details of the picture in my mind. She then told me she had received a call from him about fifteen minutes before my text indicating that he was on the run from the police in Costa Rica. She explained that his visa had expired and he lost his passport. He turned himself in to the police and was jailed.

I ended up going to Dallas to see her. It was during that visit that I shared that I was actually praying in tongues when I received the revelation about her ex-husband. She began praying in tongues and continues to this day. She has experienced amazing things as well.

One of the most powerful experiences I've had praying in tongues was one morning when I was singing in church. I could not sing the song because it was filled with words contrary to what God says. I opted to sing along quietly in tongues (Ephesians 5:19). As I did, I saw in my mind a leader of a nation (the

Lord does not want me to use his name) at his kitchen table. He was sitting, leaned over onto the table, and he was crying. His wife was trying to console him. He told her that the weight of his nation was on his shoulders. I began to weep right there. I stopped singing in tongues and began to pray in tongues. I knew the Holy Spirit was interceding for him through me and praying the perfect will of God for him.

Several weeks later, I saw this same leader on television speaking with the president of the United States. The leader stated to the president the exact same thing that I heard him say at his kitchen table in my born-again spirit when I was praying in tongues. I began to cry yet again. By the way, I am not a mushy emotional type of woman. But the tears flow from compassion that wells up on the inside of me that I know is the Holy Spirit.

I'm just a country girl living in Louisiana (I was born and raised in Texas— had to throw that in!) who loves Jesus and wants to share his goodness through the power and demonstration of the Holy Spirit. We make a really good team. He wants to team up with you too.

APPLICATION ASSIGNMENT

1. Get your Bible and read the scriptures I have listed in this section.

2. Ask the Holy Spirit to guide you into these truths.

3. Be honest with yourself. Based on the soil conditions outlined in Mark 4, which soil are you? What is the condition of your heart with respect to these seeds regarding praying in tongues?

4. If you want to pray in tongues, you can do it on your own. Or, if you need a "jump start," ask someone who prays in tongues to help you.

5. Journal your experience(s)!

Conclusion

Every believer has been created and thoroughly equipped to advance the kingdom of Jesus Christ until he returns. Unknowingly though, most churchgoers have delegated all responsibilities to their pastors and others whom God has appointed to the various offices (Ephesians 4:11). What if the military only had the officers on the battlefield with no soldiers? What if the officers were the only ones being deployed to the various countries without soldiers? A frightening visual.

It's no different in God's army. Everyone has a role and responsibility. He has made each of us a good soldier of Jesus Christ (2 Timothy 2:3). He has a kingdom to be advanced and every soldier is needed. You have a sphere of influence on the battlefield. We are incomplete without you rising up and taking your position (Ephesians 4:16). Look what Jesus says:

> *Then said he unto his disciples, The harvest truly is plenteous, but the labourers are few; pray ye therefore the Lord of the harvest, that he will send forth labourers into his harvest.* (Matthew 9:37-38)

That is you, my fellow soldier. We need you in the harvest. It's harvest time. There is work to be done for the kingdom before Jesus returns. When you stand before our King and Lord, Jesus Christ, and if he were to ask you, "What did you do with what I gave you," how would you respond? Harold asks this piercing question and I love it.

Jesus gave you: his life, his Spirit, his word, his armor, the use of his name, his power, his authority, his love, his grace, as well as dominion, provision, and an anointing, and placed you in his kingdom until he returns. This list is not all-inclusive but it gives you an idea of what has been freely given to you through the beating, death, and resurrection of Jesus Christ.

Don't limit the Holy Spirit by operating in just one area. The Holy Spirit is in you with all of his fruit and all of his gifts. Pursue all of him in your daily life. Yes, there is an order in the church assembly, but you are only there one or two days of the week. Get out of the four walls of a building and stir up the gift of the Holy Spirit who is in you (2 Timothy 1:6). He is power, he is love, and he is a sound mind that knows all things. Trust him, partner with him, and enjoy the adventure of advancing God's kingdom.

It has been an honor for me to sit under the instruction of the Holy Spirit to share these truths and experiences with you. I pray that you have a revelation of the truth that it is Christ who is in you. In the world's system I am insignificant, unknown, and would pale in comparison to many who are powerful with highly influential careers. However, in God's system I am his daughter and I have his undivided attention any time I want it. I have his DNA (2 Peter 1:4), and I have access to all that his kingdom offers at my disposal for his purpose to be fulfilled in my life and the life of others. God doesn't have favorites. This is you too!

In God's sovereignty, he has created us for relationship. He has done his part; Jesus has done his part; and now he needs us to play the part for which he has designed us. He can only accomplish his will through those who will yield to him and his word.

My prayer is that you enjoy this incredible adventurous journey with him, and step into the role that was written for you for such a time as this (Esther 4:14). We all have a part to play. It'd be a shame to let the role of your lifetime pass you by.

Grab hold of your destiny by spending time in God's word. That is the only way to know what plans God has for your life. When you do, you'll hunger for more, just like I did—more of the life-giving seeds sown into your heart.

Then start applying the word in your everyday life, and watch and see how God uses you to fulfill his plans on the earth. Your experience may be different than mine, but it will be no less fulfilling, adventurous, life-giving, and life-fulfilling. It's important you step into your specific role, for we are incomplete as a body without each person playing the part as God designed it. Enjoy the process as you go along. Remember, seed, time, and harvest. God bless you dear friend.

About the Author

Kimberly Ann Jones is the co-founder of Ezekiel's Christian Ministries, located just outside Shreveport, Louisiana. The mission of Ezekiel's is to show ordinary people that they can live extraordinary lives because of Jesus Christ and the principles of his kingdom.

Kimberly Ann is passionate about sharing the Father's love with others, and equipping believers to step out in their identity as ambassadors for Jesus Christ in God's kingdom. She leads several women's Bible studies, ministers in a women's prison, and facilitates a "Moms in Prayer" group at her son's high school. She has also participated in two mission trips with YWAM (Youth With A Mission) in the Dominican Republic teaching and equipping Christians there. Kimberly Ann's personal mission is to freely give to others as she has freely received from the Lord. She has experienced the power of Mark 4 in the Bible in her life and has witnessed the results of lives forever changed as she has discipled others on these principles.

Prior to forming the ministry with her husband, Harold, Kimberly Ann had a fulfilling career climbing the ladder in corporate America where she worked at the top two automobile insurance companies in the United States, Allstate and State Farm. Armed with a strong work ethic from an early age, Kimberly Ann was promoted to superintendent at age twenty-seven making her one of the youngest superintendents for State Farm in the state of Texas at the time.

While not raised in a church, Kimberly Ann had an awareness of Jesus during her childhood growing up in East Texas, relying on him to help her cope with a not-so-perfect upbringing. Kimberly Ann says her spiritual walk really began when she desired to know more about God when she witnessed God's word for healing manifest in her young son's body after he was diagnosed with a congenital heart condition. Her pursuit of the Lord led her to step away from the corporate world to spend more time with her son. She homeschooled him for eight years while using this precious time to immerse herself in the truths contained in the Bible.

During this season in her life, she and her husband enrolled in and graduated from Dominion Bible Institute, a division of John G. Lake Ministries. Together, they served for six years as Life Team leaders and state directors for Louisiana.

Along with running their ministry, Kimberly Ann and Harold now own Covert Energy Solutions, LLC, an energy management and LED lighting company. They started Covert with a goal of applying God's kingdom principles from Isaiah 48:17 in the operation of the business. From the design of the logo to the sales and marketing strategies, every decision is a result of input from the Holy Spirit.

Kimberly Ann warmly invites you to visit her ministry's website, EzekielsChristianMinistries.com, and to enjoy and take advantage of the resources available, including the video teachings and articles. You can connect with Kimberly Ann there, as well as through her Facebook page. She looks forward to hearing from you.